A Fiction Writer's Guide to Peace

A Fiction Writer's Guide to Peace

Crafting Nonviolent Heroism

Gabriel Ertsgaard

BLOOMSBURY ACADEMIC

LONDON · NEW YORK · OXFORD · NEW DELHI · SYDNEY

BLOOMSBURY ACADEMIC
Bloomsbury Publishing Plc, 50 Bedford Square, London, WC1B 3DP, UK
Bloomsbury Publishing Inc, 1385 Broadway, New York, NY 10018, USA
Bloomsbury Publishing Ireland, 29 Earlsfort Terrace, Dublin 2, D02 AY28, Ireland

BLOOMSBURY, BLOOMSBURY ACADEMIC and the Diana logo are trademarks
of Bloomsbury Publishing Plc

First published in Great Britain 2025

Cover design: Rebecca Heselton
Cover image: Olives © Adobe Stock

This book is dedicated to all my colleagues in the Peace and Justice Studies Association (PJSA) and the Science Fiction & Fantasy Writers Association (SFWA) who are willing to imagine worlds of hope.

CONTENTS

ACKNOWLEDGMENTS

I'd like to express my gratitude to the following: 1) My colleagues in the Kean University English Department; when I told them I'd be quitting my full-time job to write this book, rather than denouncing my folly, they congratulated me on taking the risk; 2) The staff at Bloomsbury Academic, especially my acquisitions editor Lucy Brown who worked with me for a year and a half before we even had a contract; 3) Michael Gross of the Authors Guild legal department for his very helpful contract advice; 4) The family members who insisted that I should move home to Oregon while working on this project, especially Nick and Hanna; in the midst of a global pandemic, with two young boys and a third on the way, they found room for a "live-in uncle."

Note: Portions of Chapters 2 and 7 previously appeared in the Spring 2022 issue of *The Peace Chronicle*.

1

Introduction

One evening back in 2019, I found myself browsing *MASH* memorabilia on eBay. The classic 1970s television show about US Army doctors during the Korean War holds a special place in my heart, despite its now apparent flaws, for featuring nonviolent heroism even in a wartime setting. My eBay search led to a June 1977 issue of *TV Guide* with a cover illustration of Alan Alda as Captain Hawkeye Pierce. Next to him were the words: "Here's How They're Going To Replace Violence."[1] At that point, I'd already formed the idea for the book in your hands—a guide to crafting nonviolent heroism in fiction—but it would take another year before I started writing the first draft.

The *TV Guide* issue only briefly sat on my "watch list" before I bought it. How could I resist an article on the strategies *MASH* writers used to replace violent heroism in their storytelling? When the magazine arrived, though, I discovered that the cover text and cover image pointed to two different articles. Near the back of the issue was an interview with Alan Alda. And near the front, a completely separate article on entertainment industry anti-violence efforts.

There are some good books on American pressure campaigns against television violence in the 1950s through 1980s. I've found *Target: Prime Time* by Kathryn Montgomery and *See No Evil* by

---

[1] *TV Guide* proved indecisive regarding the title of this article by Ellen Torgerson. The table of contents lists it as "What Will Replace Violence?" while the first page declares "Violence Takes a Beating" (June 4, 1977, 6–9).

Geoffrey Cowan especially informative. But just reading the *TV Guide* article was enough to give me a sense of why those efforts failed.

The television producers sought to placate the pressure groups by reducing or eliminating violent spectacle. But this often resulted in more boring versions of the same types of stories. What is a shoot-em-up without the shooting? In her *TV Guide* article, Ellen Torgerson illustrated this problem by describing her own eleven-year-old daughter's dinnertime complaints about reduced violence in police procedurals. (Torgerson also jokingly referred to her daughter as a "straight-A student with the brutish tastes of a pre-Christian Roman.") Barely five years after that article was published, two of the iconic cartoons of my childhood debuted: *G.I. Joe: A Real American Hero* and *He-Man and the Masters of the Universe*. The former featured a modern military force, whereas the latter took place on a magical planet. Despite the difference in setting, though, both cartoons depicted heroic warriors fighting the forces of evil. Violence was back—in truth, it had never left—for ratings were king.

Something stands out to me about those television anti-violence efforts. Although the writers and producers tried to replace interpersonal violence with other forms of action,[2] they didn't try replacing heroic violence with heroic nonviolence (at least, not in a widespread way). In part, this was because the television anti-violence campaigns were entangled with wider censorship efforts that also targeted foul language, sexuality, and controversial social/political topics.[3] Far from viewing *MASH* as the model for an alternative form of storytelling, conservative pressure groups saw it as emblematic of what was wrong with television.[4]

The *TV Guide* cover that first caught my attention could serve as an accidental symbol of this missed opportunity. Although the specter of violence was always present on *MASH*, violence wasn't depicted as heroic. Rather, violence and war were depicted as tragic

---

[2]Geoffrey Cowan, *See No Evil: The Backstage Battle over Sex and Violence in Television* (New York: Simon and Schuster, 1979), 257.

[3]Ibid., 32–3, 54–5.

[4]Kathryn C. Montgomery, *Target Prime Time: Advocacy Groups and the Struggle over Entertainment Television* (New York: Oxford University Press, 1989), 39.

and absurd. The heroes of that show weren't warriors, but rather trickster-healers. Over *MASH*'s eleven-year run, the draftee doctors engaged in numerous acts of nonviolent resistance toward the military establishment. Thus, at the same time that anti-violence efforts were failing, a proof of concept for nonviolent heroism was one of the most popular shows on American television. Yet despite the close proximity of anti-violence reform and nonviolent heroism on the cover of *TV Guide*, the interior gap between the articles represented a cognitive chasm.

The purpose of this book, in part, is to find a way across that gap. To be clear, this isn't a book about television, specifically. Nor is this a book about well-meaning pressure campaigns that end up flirting with censorship. Rather, this is a book about peace, nonviolence, and the craft of writing fiction. The Methodist theologian Walter Wink referred to violence as "the ethos of our times" and "the spirituality of the modern world," but he traced the "myth of redemptive violence" back to ancient mythology.[5] Wink's analysis was rooted in a core insight: the stories we tell both reflect and shape our deepest beliefs. Those beliefs influence how we act and what we consider to be possible. Seeking peace must include writing stories where peace and nonviolence are plausible.

To be fair, it's too simplistic to blame media depictions of violence for violence in the real world. The influence between art and life flows in both directions, and we don't automatically imitate everything depicted in our favorite stories. My concern, similar to Wink's, is that overindulging in violent narratives will warp what we believe works when the stakes are the highest. The solution isn't to banish tales of violent heroism (I do enjoy a good space opera or epic fantasy, even violent ones), but rather to balance them with stories where nonviolent heroism proves equally effective. This leads to three questions: 1) Is there really an imbalance between violent and nonviolent stories? 2) Can nonviolent action really prove as effective as violent action? 3) Is it possible to write compelling stories that emphasize nonviolent heroism? That third question is the main topic of this book, but we must consider the other two as well.

---

[5] Walter Wink, *Engaging the Powers: Discernment and Resistance in a World of Domination* (Minneapolis, MN: Augsburg Fortress, 1992), 13–14.

Is There Really an Imbalance?

Walter Wink *perceived* a problem with violence in sacred narratives. The 1970s pressure groups *perceived* a problem with violence in popular television shows. But are those perceptions accurate, and how do we even measure this? After all, there are many different types of stories, and not all of them promote heroic violence. In romance novels like Jane Austen's *Pride and Prejudice*, violence may be largely irrelevant to the main plot. Even in stories where violence is relevant, many feature nonviolent alternatives.

Indeed, there are certain works from diverse ages and cultures that could constitute a canon of nonviolent literature: Aristophanes' *Lysistrata*, a Greek comedy; "The Abandoned Princess," a Korean ballad; Hans Christian Andersen's "Snow Queen," a Danish fairy tale; *Lage Raho Munna Bhai*, a Bollywood musical. Yet despite the existence of these alternatives, there is still evidence that tales of violent heroism have more cultural influence than tales of nonviolent heroism.

There are a couple of possible reasons for this. First, violent tales seem to be *more popular* than their alternatives. Second, violent tales are often considered *more important*. I should give examples of what I mean for both. Although the evidence that follows is both limited and anecdotal, I hope that it helps clarify why so many people—from parent groups to theologians—perceive an imbalance in favor of heroic violence. For those who share such a perception, it's worth providing the tools to tell different types of stories.

The sociologist Will Wright once argued that a society's most popular stories reveal its underlying beliefs or core mythology. For that reason, Wright selected some of the most commercially successful Western films for archetypal analysis.[6] I won't try to replicate Wright's analysis, but we can draw inspiration from his methodology. If you skim through the Box Office Mojo list of films that have grossed more than a billion dollars worldwide, you'll

---

[6]Will Wright, *Sixguns and Society: A Structural Study of the Western* (Berkley, CA: University of California Press, 1975).

notice that the majority emphasize heroic violence.[7] Occasionally films that prioritize alternatives to violence will make this list, but they're far less prevalent.

Film is only one medium, of course, and the data from Box Office Mojo reflects the disproportionate reach and revenue of America's Hollywood movie system. Although filmgoers worldwide seem to turn to Hollywood for violent spectacle, they may "go local" for other types of stories. Ticket prices also vary around the world. However, the box office data still lends some support to the notion that tales of violent heroism are favored.

Not only are tales of violent heroism quite popular, they are often treated as more important than other types of stories. One example of this is the AP Latin exam, administered by the American nonprofit College Board.[8] Students who pass the exam can earn college credit for high school coursework. To prepare students for the exam, an AP Latin course needs to study "two of the greatest works in Latin literature: Vergil's *Aeneid* and Caesar's *Gallic War*."[9] Instructors are encouraged to include other works as well, but the two mandatory pieces are both war literature.

However, Virgil also wrote two great pastoral poems: the *Georgics* and the *Eclogues*.[10] Pairing a pastoral poem with Caesar's book would provide a more balanced view of Latin literature. No doubt subject matter helps cement the *Aeneid*'s advantage: war versus agriculture. But is war really the more significant topic? Is it really more important for human civilization? If humankind were to abolish war, we'd probably all be better off. But if agriculture were to suddenly disappear, we'd be in a lot of trouble. Considered

---

[7]Box Office Mojo, Top Lifetime Grosses, https://www.boxofficemojo.com/chart/ww_top_lifetime_gross/ (accessed September 27, 2023).

[8]In the United States, several important educational tests are administered by College Board, an independent nonprofit organization. The best known is the SAT (originally an acronym for "Scholastic Aptitude Test") whose scores are used in the admissions process at most American colleges and universities. College Board also administers subject specific AP exams (originally an acronym for "advanced placement").

[9]AP Latin, https://apcentral.collegeboard.org/courses/ap-latin (accessed June 19, 2023).

[10]The latter was actually my choice when I taught a course on Ancient Greek and Roman Literature in Translation.

in that light, it no longer seems obvious that warriors should be elevated above farmers as literary subjects. Still, on the AP Latin exam, war stories are given priority.

To be fair, literary merit isn't based entirely on the importance of the subject matter. Certain subjects make for better fiction than others. Agriculture, despite its importance, is rooted in ordinary, everyday life. On the other hand, war involves periods of conflict and transformation. The most compelling fiction, one could argue, involves transformative conflict—that is, conflict that leads to change.[11] Is violence simply the most effective method for handling transformative conflict? If so, that might explain the predominance of heroic violence in fiction. However, there's a strong case for denying violence this status. If nonviolent action is a credible alternative, that strengthens the argument for exploring how fiction writers can depict alternatives to heroic violence.

Is Nonviolent Action Effective?

Before we can determine whether or not nonviolent action is effective, I should make two clarifications about the term "nonviolence": 1) Nonviolence doesn't mean the absence of violence. Rather, it calls for a nonviolent response to the violent actions of an adversary, persecutor, or oppressor. Sometimes, these nonviolent actions will provoke a violent response, which then brings to the surface the implicit violence of the existing social order. 2) Nonviolence is never passive, but rather active and strategic. The marches, sit-ins, boycotts, strikes, fasts, and public demonstrations that are among the most common nonviolent tactics are all intended to achieve a goal through means other than violence.

But do these tactics actually work, or are other factors (including underreported violence) secretly the source of their apparent success? The title of Joseph McQuade's 2016 *Independent* article suggests such doubts: "The Forgotten Violence that Helped India Break Free of Colonial Rule." McQuade did an excellent job of

---

[11]It's worth noting, though, that Virgil wove themes of conflict and change into his pastoral poetry.

summarizing violent Indian revolutionary activities, especially from 1897 to 1919. His article offered a credible rebuttal to sanitized accounts of the Indian struggle for independence.

However, McQuade also acknowledged that the British government effectively crushed the violent revolutionaries, setting the stage for Gandhi's emergence as the face of the Indian independence movement. McQuade noted that the defeated Indian National Army "strengthened British unease" late in the colonial period, but this didn't force the British to the negotiating table.[12] Gandhi's earlier Salt March famously did, establishing the principle that the British crown would have to negotiate with Indian activists. McQuade was right in objecting to oversimplified representations of India's independence movement, but there remains a strong case for the conventional notion that nonviolent revolutionaries made the biggest difference.

There may be cycles to the interpretation of India's fight for independence. Back in 1973, political scientist Gene Sharp made the opposite complaint to McQuade's. Sharp wrote, "Where past struggles *are* remembered ... they are explained as having been unrelated to the nonviolent struggle or only partially so (as with the Gandhian struggles in India)."[13] From Sharp's perspective, the main error was attempting to explain away the effectiveness of nonviolence, rather than failing to give credit to violence.

Historical revisionism can also be deployed in favor of nonviolence, such as Sharp's take on an earlier revolt against British colonial rule—the American Revolution. Sharp identified several forms of nonviolent resistance used by American colonists in the lead-up to the Revolutionary War, including boycotts, refusal to pay taxes, refusal to obey certain laws, and the creation of "independent political institutions." According to Sharp, the American colonists shifted to armed rebellion because of their belief in the effectiveness of violence, despite the success of their nonviolent tactics. As a

---

[12]Joseph McQuade, "The Forgotten Violence that Helped India Break Free from Colonial Rule," *The Independent*, November 10, 2016, https://www.independent.co.uk/world/the-forgotten-violence-that-helped-india-break-free-from-colonial-rule-a7409066.html (accessed September 23, 2024).

[13]Gene Sharp, *Power and Struggle: The Politics of Nonviolent Action, Part One* (Boston, MA: Porter Sargent Publishers, 1973), 74.

result, those earlier nonviolent contributions have been historically overshadowed.[14]

It's impossible to guess, of course, how the American Revolution might have unfolded had it remained predominantly nonviolent. Neither violence nor nonviolence confer a guarantee of success. However, if we heed McQuade's call to give partial credit for Indian independence to violent revolutionaries, then it only seems reasonable to also consider Sharp's case regarding nonviolent contributions to American independence.

What happens, though, when we zoom out from isolated examples to look at the bigger picture? Is nonviolence really as effective as violence for bringing about significant social change? That's the question Erica Chenoweth and Maria Stephan set out to answer when they studied 627 revolutionary campaigns from across the twentieth and early twenty-first centuries. They found that violent campaigns were successful about a quarter of the time, whereas nonviolent campaigns were successful a little over half the time. The results were particularly surprising for Chenoweth who began the research project as a skeptic.[15]

That doesn't mean, however, that these numbers would hold across all times and places. Chenoweth noted that the success rate for nonviolent campaigns declined in the second decade of the twenty-first century. This may be due, in part, to a shift toward more decentralized organizational structures among activists.[16]

Furthermore, Devorah Manekin and Tamar Mitts conducted a follow-up to Chenoweth and Stephan's study, but this time factoring for ethnicity. Manekin and Mitts found that the advantage of nonviolent campaigns over violent ones disappeared for ethnic minorities oppressed by ethnic majorities. That's because majority populaces tended to perceive civil resistance by ethnic minorities as violent and threatening, even when nonviolent tactics were used. Manekin and Mitts suggested that more research was

---

[14]Gene Sharp, *The Dynamics of Nonviolent Action: The Politics of Nonviolent Action, Part Three* (Boston, MA: Porter Sargent Publishers, 1973), 4, 495.

[15]Erica Chenoweth, *Civil Resistance: What Everyone Needs to Know* (New York: Oxford University Press, 2021), xix–xxi, 13–14.

[16]Ibid., xxii–xxiii.

needed on whether this problem could be neutralized through multi-ethnic coalitions.[17]

This is an important and troubling finding, but it only reduces nonviolence to parity with violence. That's a far cry from the premise that violence is "the only way" or even what usually works best. Indeed, if nonviolent civil resistance is depicted more widely and effectively in popular narratives, it may become harder to misrepresent the activities of nonviolent activists (or at least, to sell such misrepresentations to the public). Of course, that's just speculation at this point. Before we can find out if my supposition holds true, we must create "facts on the ground"—or more accurately, fables on the page.

Are Stories of Nonviolent Heroism Compelling?

We now come to the third question and the heart of this book—can nonviolent heroism really prove as compelling as violent heroism in fiction? My hypothesis is that, yes, it can. Nonetheless, I'll admit that it's possible for me to be wrong. It's possible that heroic violence generates a level of excitement that nonviolent alternatives simply cannot match—at least not consistently. It's possible that violent heroism allows for greater narrative efficiency, making it easier to write well. And it's possible that these and other factors add up to an insurmountable, cumulative advantage for violent heroism in fiction.

However, there's an alternate explanation for the lower profile of nonviolence in fiction: perhaps we simply lack a clear sense of how to craft such stories. For tales of violent heroism, our toolbox of tropes and structures is rooted in literature that goes back centuries. Not only that, but these stories have often been presented to us as the most important ones ever told. (Think of epic heroes like Odysseus and Beowulf.) Although we can find models of nonviolent

---

[17]Devorah Manekin and Tamar Mitts, "Effective for Whom? Ethnic Identity and Nonviolent Resistance," *American Political Science Review* 116, no. 1 (2022), 161–80, https://doi.org/10.1017/S0003055421000940.

heroism in literature if we dig for them, they are less pervasive, less celebrated, and thus their lessons are far less instinctual.

So how do we figure out which it is—an innate disadvantage for nonviolent storytelling or a lack of specialized craft knowledge? I think we can only answer that question by putting the matter to the test. My approach is to develop writing principles and strategies tailored toward nonviolent heroism. If I'm right and the problem is a lack of specialized craft knowledge, then writers will be able to use these tools to create compelling stories that engage audiences. If I'm wrong, then tales of nonviolent heroism will fail to gain ground compared to tales of violent heroism. My hypothesis will be discredited, if not outright falsified.

That's the same risk, though, that a scientist takes who dedicates their life to a bold research path—the risk that their labor will amount to mapping a dead end. Such efforts are necessary for the advancement of knowledge, but that can be a bleak consolation. I benefit, at least, from a difference between art and science. Correctly formulated scientific laws are presumably universal, but aesthetic tastes can diverge greatly. Despite my attention to popularity above, not everything that counts in art requires mass appeal. If my ideas prove useful to other writers, and their stories find small but appreciative audiences, then my work will still have some value. I hope for more, of course, but only time will tell.

At this point, a question may be pushing forward in your mind: What are these ideas, specifically, for reforming fiction writing practice? I can best answer that question by briefly previewing the remainder of this book.

Chapter 2 introduces several areas of peace studies,[18] including peace education, nonviolent civil resistance, and conflict transformation. We've already considered the second, but this chapter places nonviolent civil resistance in a broader context. This provides a modest introduction to peace studies for those unfamiliar with the field. I also propose the concept of "peace poetics" in this chapter. "Poetics" refers to a theory of writing craft, thus "peace poetics" seems an appropriate term for the intersection of peace

---

[18]The field is variously called "peace studies," "peace and conflict studies," and "peace and justice studies." I treat these terms as equivalent in this book, so my choice of term is generally guided by the context of a particular section.

studies with writing theory. Although this chapter primarily focuses on explaining concepts, it lays a foundation for the craft advice of the following four chapters.

Chapter 3 focuses on character arcs. The debate over whether plot or character should take priority in fiction writing has raged since Aristotle's time. By emphasizing character arcs, though, we can bring plot and character together. If we look closely at some of the craft advice on this topic, we find intriguing similarities to certain concepts from conflict transformation theory. Distinguishing between a fictional character's "wants and needs" has parallels to distinguishing between "interests and positions" when negotiating a conflict. This resonance creates an opportunity for bringing conflict transformation theory into the construction of character arcs. This may help writers construct characters who are internally capable of nonviolent heroism.

Chapter 4 focuses on campaigns. This chapter unpacks one big idea—namely, that caper stories (a subgenre of crime fiction) provide a structural model for nonviolent campaigns in fiction. A caper story generally features a heist or a con, and the thrill comes from watching the protagonists outwit and outmaneuver their opponents. There are several common elements of caper stories that are transferable to the depiction of nonviolent campaigns: 1) the centrality of a clever scheme (the civil resistance campaign); 2) underdogs as protagonists; 3) assembling a diverse team; 4) previewing complications that pay off when the scheme unfolds; 5) the execution of the scheme in the third act; and 6) surprising twists at the end. A writer wishing to depict compelling nonviolent campaigns would do well to study the narrative structure of caper stories.

Chapter 5 focuses on duels. In particular, it suggest three strategies for subverting heroic duels in interesting and creative ways: substitution, intervention, and nonresistance. In the first, the writer presents an alternate activity at a point in the story where a duel might be expected. For example, stage combat replaces real combat in Kenneth Grahame's "The Reluctant Dragon." In the second strategy, intervention, a third party interferes with the duel. Although this third party is often a more powerful figure than the duel participants, there are also examples of less powerful figures disrupting duels in fiction. The third strategy, nonresistance, may be the trickiest. One party in the duel must refuse to fight back, but in a manner that shows principle and courage. By doing so, they can bring down a social sanction upon their violent adversary. All three of these strategies have been used in compelling narrative works.

Chapter 6 focuses on world building in fiction. This concept is especially popular in speculative fiction circles, but it applies to all fiction writing, even stories ostensibly set in the "real" world. The grim New York of film noir, after all, isn't really the same place as the bright New York of a comic Broadway musical—and neither of these is the real New York City. They're both fictional worlds, and they're created through a writer's choices. While world building can cover everything from magic systems to political systems, this chapter digs down to an even more fundamental level. What are the mythic forces or cosmic laws that govern a particular story? These shape what is plausible or even possible in the story world.

To return to our New York example, a grim noir world would be governed by a law of decay, versus a bright Broadway world's law of renewal. A happy ending would be far more likely in the latter. A writer's choices on this front are often instinctual, but we can prime the pump for heroic nonviolence by keeping three "cosmic powers" in mind: love, persuasion, and reconciliation. This chapter is a bit conceptual since it deals with the ideas and assumptions that lie behind fictional worlds—but if you absorb its lessons, then you should have a much easier time crafting stories of nonviolent heroism.

Chapter 7 reverses the arrow, so to speak. The main focus of this book is on how peace studies concepts can be useful for fiction writers. However, this chapter looks at how peace poetics can prove valuable to activists. It especially draws on a pair of concepts from creative writing studies: creative literacy and counternarrative. The concept of "creative literacy" explores how creative skills and thinking can be applied beyond the bounds of traditional creative writing. Certainly, there's plenty of use for creative skills in peace and social justice activism. The concept of "counternarrative" explores how alternative narratives can challenge and subvert dominant cultural narratives. This is, in fact, the primary purpose of the field of narrative change work. This field already makes use of some basic literary concepts. There's still a need, though, to translate more advanced writing and literature concepts into terminology that would be useful for narrative change activists.

After spending the book advocating for peace and nonviolence, I conclude (perhaps surprisingly) with a warning against pacifist purity in fiction writing. A writer can easily get stuck by trying to be too perfect. A *mostly* nonviolent story that you can finish writing is a greater contribution than a *completely* nonviolent story that you can't. There are numerous ways to partially implement the ideas from this book, and doing so may be useful as you build new writing muscles.

What This Book Is

By now, you probably have a sense of what kind of book this is. This isn't a primer on nonviolent movements, nor a monograph of literary theory, nor even a general guide to fiction writing. Rather, this is a supplementary text with a specialized focus: how to integrate nonviolent heroism into fiction across genres. This is also only an initial work on the topic. I'm laying out a few ideas that I hope prove useful to working writers, while advancing the conversation. A special caution to academic literary critics: I don't offer comprehensive interpretations of the literary works used as examples. Rather, I focus on those features of the works that illustrate specific points or writing techniques. Otherwise, this text would quickly lose its function as an accessible writers' guide.[19]

What follows isn't intended as a paint-by-numbers system. I personally don't find those very useful as creative writing aids. Instead, I treat the writing books on my shelf as repositories of useful ideas and suggestions, not binding lawbooks. In that spirit, this book offers 1) a framework for thinking about nonviolence and fiction writing, and 2) practical suggestions and writing prompts. To use an imperfect metaphor, this book is like a trampoline: if it does its job, you won't simply stand on it, you'll leap off in a new direction.

---

[19]As an academic literary critic myself, I've had to aggressively rein in the impulse to delve deeper than is appropriate for this project.

2

From Peace Studies to Peace Poetics

Peace studies is a diverse field, and a complete survey of the scholarship falls outside the scope of this book. In this chapter, though, we'll take a closer look at several important topics in the field—namely, peace education, civil resistance, and conflict transformation. Furthermore, we'll explore how these topics connect to literature and creative writing. To put it another way, this chapter links peace studies to peace poetics.

What do I mean by "peace poetics"? Let's start with the second word, "poetics." It originally comes from the Greek word for making or crafting. Aristotle used this term for the craft of creative writing in his *Poetics*. Now, words have a tendency to slide around in meaning over the course of centuries, especially if they cross between languages. That's why we also have the word "poetry" for a specific type of creative writing. But "poetics" can analyze any type of verbal or narrative art.[1]

Portions of this chapter previously appeared in the following article: Gabriel Ertsgaard, "Solarpunk and Peace Poetics," *The Peace Chronicle* 14, no. 2 (Spring 2022), 40–5.

[1] The Merriam-Webster and University of Chicago websites have interesting articles on this topic. "A Poet by any Other Name," Merriam-Webster.com, https://www.merriam-webster.com/words-at-play/the-history-of-the-word-poet (accessed October 14, 2022). Rad Borislavov, "Poetics," The Chicago School of Media Theory, University of Chicago, https://csmt.uchicago.edu/glossary2004/poetics.htm (accessed October 14, 2022).

So how does peace come into this? I use the term "peace poetics" for exploring how to craft certain types of stories—namely, those that promote nonviolent conflict transformation and the possibility of peace. These aren't passive stories. Rather, nonviolent civil resistance is a form of heroic action, an alternative to heroic violence. Also, different aspects of peace and conflict studies may serve the needs of different stories. For example, a story that focuses on conflict transformation might not feature civil resistance.

In addition to introducing these core peace studies concepts, I'll analyze two stories later in this chapter, both from *The Weight of Light: A Collection of Solar Futures*.[2] In this interdisciplinary project, speculative fiction writers teamed up with scientists and other scholars to imagine a range of future societies, all based on plausible solar power technologies. The first story, "For the Snake of Power" by Brenda Cooper, offers an example of civil resistance. The second, "Big Rural" by Cat Rambo, offers an example of conflict transformation. By examining how these stories work, we can get a taste of what peace poetics might accomplish. However, before turning to civil resistance and conflict transformation, let's first look at peace education.

Peace Education

In *The Little Book of Strategic Peacebuilding*, Lisa Schirch outlined four cornerstones of her topic: 1) waging conflict nonviolently, 2) reducing direct violence, 3) transforming relationships, and 4) building capacity.[3] We'll take a closer look at "waging conflict nonviolently" and "transforming relationships" later in this chapter, but for now let's focus on "building capacity."

One way to build a society's capacity for peace is through education. According to Schirch, "Peace education explores the causes of conflict and conditions of peace." She also advocated educating people about human rights and environmental issues in

---

[2] Joey Eschrich and Clark A. Miller (eds.), *The Weight of Light: A Collection of Solar Futures* (Tempe, AZ: Arizona State University, 2018).
[3] Lisa Schirch, *The Little Book of Strategic Peacebuilding* (Intercourse, PA: Good Books, 2004), 25–7.

order to promote peacebuilding. Schirch further noted the practical skills that can be learned through conflict transformation training. Finally, she highlighted how "peace media" can "provide objective information about violent conflicts … and increase awareness about peaceful alternatives."[4]

Fictional stories can contribute to peacebuilding in a way that resonates with peace education, but for most works of fiction, there are also important differences. Yes, there's such a thing as instructional fiction. For example, the popular Magic School Bus series, first created by Joanna Cole and Bruce Degen in the 1980s, uses fictional stories to educate children about science. Certainly, someone could create a similar series for peace education. Most fiction, though, doesn't try to teach an explicit curriculum. The first priority isn't the lesson, but rather the story.

How might non-instructional fiction help build a society's capacity for peace? Fiction, I believe, affects our matrix of imagination. That is, the stories we consume help shape the worlds we can imagine. If fictional stories are dominated by violent heroism, it becomes harder to conceive of nonviolent alternatives. If fictional worlds are filled with tragedy, it becomes harder to embrace hope. Stories of nonviolent heroism and conflict transformation, on the other hand, lay a narrative foundation for peace education. Fiction can contribute to peacebuilding by making peace imaginable.

This is certainly true for the writers of such stories. The very process of crafting stories in which conflict is peaceably transformed may help writers imagine nonviolent possibilities for their own lives and world. An instructor could even weave fiction writing assignments into a peace studies curriculum with this goal in mind. For such an assignment, it might not matter whether the final story proved compelling to an external audience. After all, the primary purpose of that assignment would be raising the writer's own consciousness. However, this book aims beyond writing for personal development to the tricky task of writing for an audience. As such, we must also consider the ability of fiction to influence an audience's imagination.

In fact, instructors across educational levels have recognized the potential for teaching peace through literature. Poet and English professor Jeff Gundy addressed this topic in his essay "Literature,

---

[4] Ibid., 57–8.

Nonviolence, and Nonviolent Teaching" from the 2003 book *Teaching Peace: Nonviolence and the Liberal Arts*. Gundy observed that the archetypal hero in American literature is an individualistic, violent figure. But Gundy also identified a consistent countercurrent in the American canon: a distrust for the heroic archetype. He insisted that this critique of violent heroism lay at the heart of many great literary works, from Melville's *Moby Dick* to the Western classic *Shane*. Gundy acknowledged that both his criticism and pedagogy were rooted in a philosophy of Christian nonviolence. Nonetheless, he didn't expect to convert his students to pacifism. For Gundy, it was enough to guide them toward looking at the dominant model of heroic violence more critically, which then allowed his students to imagine a wider range of alternatives.[5]

A decade later, Candace C. Carter and Linda Pickett collaborated on *Youth Literature for Peace Education*. In contrast to Gundy's focus on higher education, Carter and Pickett's book focused on primary education. They recognized an opportunity to bring peace education into public schools as an extension of civic education. Carter and Pickett argued that learning how to be a good citizen should include learning how to solve conflicts within a society peacefully. Such a curriculum could explore various facets of peace: "harmonious living," "conflict prevention," "avoidance and repair of harm," "fulfillment of needs," and "social and legal justice." The lessons of peace education could also be extended to international contexts, encouraging a concept of global citizenship.[6] Carter and Pickett contended that literature is a useful vehicle for the development of both language skills and social literacy. If the right works are chosen, youth literature can help students develop a vocabulary for handling conflict and expressing their needs. Such works also provide opportunities for students to reflect on the underlying causes of conflicts and their possible resolution.[7]

Admittedly, the contributions of Gundy, Carter, and Pickett veer closer to peace criticism than peace poetics. That is, their efforts

---

[5]Jeff Gundy, "Literature, Nonviolence, and Nonviolent Teaching," *Teaching Peace: Nonviolence and the Liberal Arts*, ed. J. Denny Weaver and Gerald Biesecker-Mast (New York: Rowman & Littlefield, 2003), 125–6.
[6]Candice C. Carter and Linda Pickett, *Youth Literature for Peace Education* (New York: Palgrave Macmillan, 2014), 1–5.
[7]Ibid., 20–2.

are more focused on the consumption of creative literature than its production. Even so, peace education offers a useful template for fiction writers. Writers can also learn important lessons by reading stories carefully. For writers, though, it's important to pay attention to craft details. What makes a particular conflict and its resolution compelling? What makes it believable? How is the story structured? These questions move us from reading to writing, so we must shift our focus onto specific types of action that can be depicted in literature. In particular, let's now explore two areas of peace studies that will prove important for later chapters in this book: civil resistance and conflict transformation.

Civil Resistance

One of Schirch's cornerstones of strategic peacebuilding is "waging conflict nonviolently." Common equivalent terms include "nonviolent direct action" and "civil resistance." This terminological congestion has a long history in pacifist thought. As Theodore Paullin explained in his 1944 *Introduction to Non-Violence*:

> The very diversity of terms used to describe the pacifist position shows that none of them satisfactorily express the essence of pacifist philosophy. Among those commonly used are: (1) non-resistance, (2) passive resistance, (3) non-violent resistance, (4) super-resistance, (5) non-violent non-cooperation, (6) civil disobedience, (7) non-violent coercion, (8) non-violent direct action, (9) war without violence, and (10) Satyagraha or soul force.[8]

As Paullin acknowledged, some activists of his time viewed pacifism as a morally binding life philosophy, whereas others saw it as a pragmatically useful toolset for social change. Although the two approaches aren't exclusive, this distinction still appears in the present century. For example, Mark Kurlansky emphasized the former in *Nonviolence: The History of a Dangerous Idea*,

---

[8]Theodore Paullin, *Introduction to Non-Violence* (Philadelphia, PA: The Pacifist Research Bureau, 1944), 6.

whereas Erica Chenoweth insisted on the latter in *Civil Resistance: What Everyone Needs to Know*.[9] Nonetheless, many contemporary activists would agree with Paullin that the two approaches "in practice … find themselves united in their logical condemnation on violence as an effective means for bringing about social change."[10]

Certain terms were already passing out of favor when Paullin wrote his pamphlet. He noted that most pacifists had abandoned the once popular designation of "non-resistants," in part because the latter implied passivity, not active efforts for peace and justice. Ironically, "pacifism" would itself eventually suffer the same discredit.[11] In 1973, Gene Sharp claimed, "Nonviolent action is thus not synonymous with 'pacifism,'" though he acknowledged that pacifists could at least engage in nonviolent action.[12] In 2006, Kurlansky assumed a sharper division when he wrote, "Pacifism is passive; but nonviolence is active."[13] Fifteen years later, a similar charge was leveled against "nonviolence." As Chenoweth explained in her 2021 book, "I've avoided the term 'nonviolent' in the title because many people tend to interpret that term as equivalent to words like 'passive,' 'submissive,' 'inactive,' 'peaceful,' or 'resigned'."[14]

Although I agree with Chenoweth that "civil resistance" has a better chance than "pacifism" or "nonviolence" of escaping those connotations of passivity, the problem does not lie entirely within the realm of word choice. Rather, for many people it may seem implausible or even subversive to claim that viable alternatives to violence exist. Both Kurlansky and Judith Butler suggested that the very concept of nonviolence is a threat to entrenched political powers, insofar as it undermines the credibility of state-sanctioned violence.[15] This would help explain Paullin's decades-old observation

---

[9]Mark Kurlansky, *Nonviolence: The History of a Dangerous Idea* (New York: Modern Library, 2006). Erica Chenoweth, *Civil Resistance: What Everyone Needs to Know* (New York: Oxford University Press, 2021).

[10]Paullin, *Introduction to Non-Violence*, 5.

[11]Ibid.

[12]Gene Sharp, *Power and Struggle: The Politics of Nonviolent Action, Part One* (Boston, MA: Porter Sargent Publishers, 1973), 68.

[13]Kurlansky, *Nonviolence*, 6.

[14]Chenoweth, *Civil Resistance*, 6.

[15]Judith Butler, *The Force of Nonviolence: An Ethico-Political Bind* (New York: Verso, 2020).

that "opponents of pacifism have hastened to define [terms] in such a way as to deny validity to the pacifist philosophy."[16]

To put it another way, we may have a "toilet" problem on our hands. Over the course of centuries, the meaning of the word "toilet" changed from a cloth used for personal grooming, to the room in which grooming and bathing occur, to a polite euphemism (going to the toilet) for another bodily process occurring in the same room (defecation), to the device into which one defecates.[17] At that point, "toilet" was doomed. As Jan Freeman observed in an article for the *Boston Globe*, "Euphemisms, however, are famous for their fragility. ... once the unspeakable fixture acquired the name of toilet, the genteel uses of toilet were in danger."[18] In a similar manner, there is the danger that any term for "nonviolent action" or "civil resistance" may acquire the "stench" of passivity. This unfortunate tendency is rooted in an intuitive but false binary: because violence is coded as active, alternatives to violence get coded as passive.

One of the tasks of peace poetics is to challenge this false binary. The more that stories about civil resistance circulate, the easier it will be for people to imagine active alternatives to violence. The better we understand how to tell such stories, the easier it will be to put them into circulation. Of course, for writers to craft such stories, we also need to know something about the methods of civil resistance campaigns. Let's now consider efforts to codify knowledge on that topic.

Gene Sharp's 1973 three-volume opus *The Politics of Nonviolent Action* laid the foundation for subsequent work in nonviolence theory. Sharp challenged the top-down, monolithic conception of power. Rather, he argued that power is essentially bottom up and distributed.[19] Sharp pointed out that even the most powerful rulers rely on others to carry out their commands. Thus, there are numerous ways in which those governed can withdraw their cooperation, and not all of these require the use of violent force.[20]

---

[16]Paullin, *Introduction to Non-Violence*, 6.

[17]"How the Toilet Got Its Name," Merriam-Webster.com, https://www.merriam-webster.com/words-at-play/word-history-of-toilet (accessed October 14, 2022).

[18]Jan Freeman, "Toile and Trouble," *The Boston Globe*, October 13, 2002.

[19]Sharp, *Power and Struggle*, 8–10.

[20]Ibid., 24–5; Gene Sharpe, *The Methods of Nonviolent Action: The Politics of Nonviolent Action, Part Two* (Boston: Porter Sargent Publishers, 1973), 113–15.

Disobedience to unjust laws, economic disengagement, and the creation of alternative communication channels (independent media) all undermine centralized power.

Sharp referred to the use of nonviolent tactics as "political *jiu-jitsu*," and we can understand what he was getting at by thinking of violent suppression as a logistical problem. To violently crush nonviolent dissenters, a government must have sufficient security forces to handle the scale of the dissent. It must also maintain the loyalty of those forces, which isn't always guaranteed. Furthermore, the government must suppress dissenters without triggering a backlash that deepens the resistance. Violence alone cannot accomplish all of these things. Yet a regime incapable of obtaining sufficient cooperation from its populace will ultimately fall.[21] Even if political power is, in theory, concentrated at the top of a pyramid, in practice it is constantly being renegotiated. Thus, Sharp argued that actual political power is rooted in the consent of the governed, though he acknowledged that this consent is often obtained under duress.[22]

Mark and Paul Engler recognized Sharp's importance in their 2016 book *This Is an Uprising: How Nonviolent Revolt Is Shaping the Twenty-first Century*. However, they also emphasized ways in which subsequent activists revised Sharp's theory of power, in particular by adding the "pillars of support" concept. These later activists preserved Sharp's precept that power ultimately resides with the general population, as well as his understanding that the general population is made up of individuals. However, they emphasized an intermediary level of social organization. People organize themselves into institutions—religious communities, business communities, media, security forces, etc.—and these institutions serve as pillars of support for the existing social order. To change the social order requires knocking down those pillars of support by turning the institutions to the side of the reformers or revolutionaries. When enough pillars fall, so will the target, whether it is an oppressive government or an unjust law.[23]

---

[21]Sharpe, *Power and Struggle*, 34–6.
[22]Ibid., 26–30.
[23]Mark Engler and Paul Engler, *This Is an Uprising: How Nonviolent Revolt Is Shaping the Twenty-first Century* (New York: Nation Books, 2016), 91–2.

Yet skeptics might still ask, are these methods really as effective as violence? Are the success stories normative, or rare exceptions? To answer these questions, we must circle back to some of the research discussed in this book's introduction. In *Civil Resistance: What Everyone Needs to Know*, political scientist Erica Chenoweth admitted to having started as one of those skeptics. Together with fellow political scientist Maria Stephan, though, she set out to find some answers. They analyzed mass movements from around the globe from 1900–2006. All of these movements sought significant change at the national level. After running the numbers, the results were stark: The nonviolent movements proved to be more than twice as successful as the violent ones.[24]

That doesn't guarantee, of course, that the results would be the same at every point in history. Nor did the dataset include smaller, local campaigns. Also, as noted in the introduction to this book, ethnic bias can influence the reception of nonviolent campaigns.[25] Nonetheless, these results at least established a baseline credibility for nonviolent action. Civil resistance works in real life. That doesn't mean nonviolence is 100 percent effective, but neither is violence. (It's surprising how often the latter point slips from people's minds.) This book, though, is concerned with a different question. Can civil resistance work in a fictional story, one that grips a reader? A later chapter will address this topic in detail, but for now, let's look at one story as a case study: "For the Snake of Power" by Brenda Cooper.

Case Study: "For the Snake of Power"

"For the Snake of Power"[26] begins as an amateur detective story. The protagonist, Rosa, is a power company employee in a future version of Phoenix, Arizona. A massive dust storm has damaged

---

[24]Chenoweth, *Civil Resistance*, xix–xxi, 13–14.

[25]Devorah Manekin and Tamar Mitts, "Effective for Whom? Ethnic Identity and Nonviolent Resistance," *American Political Science Review* 116, no. 1 (2022), 161–80, https://doi.org/10.1017/S0003055421000940.

[26]Brenda Cooper, "For the Snake of Power," *The Weight of Light: A Collection of Solar Futures*, ed. Joey Eschrich and Clark A. Miller (Tempe, AZ: Arizona State University, 2018), 43–59.

the "snake," an enormous solar array that provides the city with power. The resulting brownouts leave poorer residents without A/C during triple-digit heat. In some cases, this proves deadly. But more power is missing than the damage can explain, so Rosa goes digging for answers. With the help of the AI program HANNA, she finds them. Rosa and HANNA discover that the Arizona governor has agreed to sell off 20 percent of their power out of state, and that contract takes priority over local needs. No contingency has been made for emergencies. Both Rosa's supervisor and her best friend Callie insist that nothing can be done. The problem is way above their paygrade.

Cooper could have stopped there with a hopeless, Chinatown-style ending. ("Forget it, Jake. It's the Association of Solar Power.") This is a solarpunk story, though, a genre that tries to provide more optimistic visions of the future than its older cousin, cyberpunk. Instead of nihilistic closure, Cooper pivoted from the detective story to a related genre—the caper story. This fits with one of my core ideas about peace poetics: caper stories offer a structural model for portraying civil resistance campaigns in fiction. (We'll explore this topic in the chapter on "campaigns.")

How does a caper story work? First, you come up with a scheme, usually a heist or a con. You assemble a colorful cast of characters, each with unique skills. Then you put the scheme into action and see if they pull it off. (These stories also features growth arcs, complications, etc., but those elements aren't unique to the genre.) In a story featuring nonviolent heroism, a civil resistance campaign can serve as the scheme. That's why caper stories offer a model for narrative structure.

Indeed, this is exactly what we see in "For the Snake of Power." Rosa tells Inez, a friend from her old neighborhood, what's going on. Inez convinces Rosa to turn whistleblower and connects her with underground media contacts. Local activists use this coverage as a springboard to call for mass protests. These spread throughout the city, even to better-off neighborhoods, with residents demanding the governor's resignation. This draws the attention of the major news channels. Or to put it another way, the pillars of support for the governor's administration start to fall.

Although Rosa is the point-of-view character, she isn't actually the lead organizer for this civil resistance campaign. Rather, Inez and her contacts quickly organize things once they discover that Rosa is willing to turn whistleblower. For that reason, much of the planning happens behind the scenes. Rosa is a catalyst for the widespread resistance, but she doesn't have a granular view of how the campaign is organized. Nonetheless, the basic elements of a caper story are there: coming up with a scheme, assembling a diverse cast of characters with unique skills, putting the scheme into action.

The story even has a surprise twist at the end, a common feature of caper stories. Rosa's friend Callie shows up at the protest. She reveals that, with the help of the AI HANNA, she has shut down the transmission line sending power out of state. Rather than admit that their AI went rogue, the governor must save face by claiming to have made the decision herself, thus ending the brownouts. Although their actions cost both Rosa and Callie their jobs, the civil resistance efforts prove effective. Cooper's Phoenix may not be a utopia, but it isn't a dystopia either. Like the solarpunk genre as a whole, the story insists on the credibility of hope.

In real life, it's important to acknowledge, campaigns like this one don't accomplish their goals in a single day. Rather, the road to victory takes months or even years. As George Lakey put it in *How We Win: A Guide to Direct Action Campaigning*, "The trouble is, when I look back on the one-off protests I've joined over the years, I don't remember a single one that changed the policy we were protesting."[27] Lakey insisted that individual protests needed to be embedded in larger campaigns to get results. However, this sort of narrative condensation is a common literary device. Take the movie *Love, Actually*, wherein characters learn new languages, learn new instruments, and fall deeply in love in under a month.[28] These are real life activities, but presented on an abridged timeline. The

---

[27]George Lakey, *How We Win: A Guide to Direct Action Campaigning* (New York: Melville House, 2018), 4.
[28]*Love, Actually*, directed by Richard Curtis (Universal Pictures, 2003).

same is true for the events in "For the Snake of Power." Although the timeline is very condensed, the elements of civil resistance are believable.

Conflict Transformation

There are several other terms for what I've designated "conflict transformation"—most notably, "conflict resolution," "conflict management," and "alternative dispute resolution." In some cases, the choice of terms is governed by context. Take the last of those terms, "alternative dispute resolution." This refers to alternatives to using a formal judicial process. That is, disputants might opt for mediation or arbitration, rather than settling things in court. This term is most common in the legal profession where the court system can be treated as the default norm. Hence, Jacqueline M. Nolan-Haley's *Alternative Dispute Resolution in a Nutshell* is intended for an audience of lawyers.[29]

In other cases, the choice of terms may reflect a philosophical position. In *The Little Book of Conflict Transformation*, John Paul Lederach laid out the case for his preferred term, contra popular alternatives like "conflict resolution" or "conflict management." Lederach found that some disputants were leery of the term "conflict resolution." They were concerned that focusing too much on the end goal (resolution) could result in giving the root causes of conflict insufficient attention. Lederach began using the term "conflict transformation" to describe his process, as "transformation" better captured a sense of deep, constructive change.[30] Although "conflict resolution" was the term used in my own peace studies coursework, I find Lederach's argument compelling, so I've adopted "conflict transformation" as the preferred term for this book.

---

[29]Jacqueline M. Nolan-Haley, *Alternative Dispute Resolution in a Nutshell*, 4th ed. (St. Paul, MN: West Academic Publishing, 2013).
[30]John Paul Lederach, *The Little Book of Conflict Transformation* (New York: Good Books, 2003), 3–6.

In *Challenging Conflict: Mediation Through Understanding*, Gary Friedman and Jack Himmelstein explained that conflicts often turn into downward spirals. Disputants don't know how to escape the conflict, even if all sides want to. Entrenched positions, misunderstandings, and lack of trust accumulate in a "conflict trap."[31]

The field of conflict transformation, regardless of one's preferred term, focuses on helping people escape conflict traps. This is certainly true of *Getting to Yes: Negotiating Agreement Without Giving In*, one of the field's most influential classics. (First written by Roger Fisher and William Ury in 1981, the second and third editions were co-authored by Bruce Patton.) They propose a four-part method for constructive negotiations: 1) "separate people from the problem," 2) "focus on interests, not positions," 3) "invent options for mutual gain," and 4) "insist on using objective criteria."[32] Used effectively, this method can redirect disputants out of conflict traps by helping them make concrete progress toward resolving their issues.

Although primarily a negotiation manual, concepts from *Getting to Yes* have proven of great value to conflict transformation professionals. Consider *The Mediation Process: Practical Strategies for Resolving Conflict* by Christopher W. Moore. The intended audience for this book is neutral, third-party mediators. Professional mediators help parties in conflict work through their disputes and find solutions that everyone involved can accept. Unlike arbitrators, mediators don't issue rulings or make binding decisions. Rather, they help people in conflict find their own solutions.[33] Moore's book is peppered with concepts from *Getting to Yes*, including the aforementioned distinction between interests and positions.

---

[31] Gary Friedman and Jack Himmelstein, *Challenging Conflict: Mediation Through Understanding* (Chicago, IL: American Bar Association, 2008), xxv–xxvii. Throughout their book, Friedman and Himmelstein alternate between stories of conflicts they've mediated and commentary sections exploring key conflict transformation concepts. This blend of narrative and expository material is itself intriguing from a peace poetics perspective. However, a rhetorical study of *Challenging Conflict* must wait for another time, as it falls outside the scope of this brief survey.

[32] Roger Fisher, William Ury, and Bruce Patton, *Getting to Yes: Negotiating Agreement Without Giving In*, 3rd ed. (New York: Penguin Books, 2011), 17.

[33] Christopher W. Moore, *The Mediation Process: Practical Strategies for Resolving Conflict*, 4th ed. (San Francisco, CA: Jossey-Bass, 2014), 8–11.

However, it also walks through every step of running a mediation session, going well beyond the scope of the negotiation classic.

Although it's possible to depict a mediation session in fiction, that's probably not the most engaging way to draw on conflict transformation concepts. Nonetheless, solving the puzzle of how to overcome a seemingly intractable conflict could prove compelling, as long as the resolution isn't rushed. Furthermore, if a character goes through a growth arc as they move through the conflict transformation process it's a recipe for strong, character-driven fiction. The next chapter will explore this option in detail. For now, though, let's consider a single case study of how conflict transformation concepts can contribute to fictional narratives: Cat Rambo's "Big Rural."

Case Study: "Big Rural"

"Big Rural"[34] also begins with a mystery. The protagonist, Trish Soledad, returns to Tierra del Ray, her hometown in rural Arizona. Like Rosa from "For the Snake of Power," Trish works for a power company that is unpopular with local residents. Sol Dominion has planted a massive solar farm on the outskirts of town and intends to roll out an even larger phase two. The plant, though, has suffered serious vandalism, and the culprits haven't been caught. If the problem continues, it could jeopardize the project. Trish's future with Sol Dominion depends on her ability to stop the vandalism.

Neither local law enforcement nor the solar farm security guards show much interest in helping Trish solve the mystery. Nonetheless, she eventually realizes that her high school boyfriend, Jeff, is the ringleader of the vandals. But Trish also realizes that Sol Dominion hasn't taken local concerns into account. The solar farm itself is considered an eyesore that ruins the view from their favorite bluff. Why would they want to see it expanded? The shift to solar power coincided with the shutdown of the local coal plant, one of the

---

[34]Cat Rambo, "Big Rural," *The Weight of Light: A Collection of Solar Futures*, ed. Joey Eschrich and Clark A. Miller (Tempe, AZ: Arizona State University, 2018), 107–20.

small town's largest employers. Finally, Sol Dominion's acquisition of water rights threatens to crowd out agriculture.

At the end of the story, Trish and Jeff meet atop the bluff. He knows that she's figured things out and waits for the metaphorical hammer to drop. Instead, Trish surprises him. She's cashed in all her favors at Sol Dominion to arrange a change in the phase two design. "Ever heard of agro-voltaics?" she asks Jeff, "Imagine crops growing between the panels, sheltered from some of the heat."[35] Now the space will be dual purpose, benefitting both the power company and the community. Rather than a black hole, the view from the bluff will look down on a giant garden.

This solution illustrates one of those key ideas from *Getting to Yes*, the distinction between interests and positions. Basically, a "position" is whatever the parties on each side of a conflict are demanding. The position of the power company is that phase two needs to proceed without interference. The position of the vandals is that this expansion must be stopped. An "interest" is whatever needs or wants the parties are trying to accomplish through their positions. By looking a level deeper, Trish finds an alternative that addresses everyone's needs.

Indeed, pushing through this alternative is Trish's key heroic act in "Big Rural." The closest thing to civil resistance in the story is Jeff's vandalism campaign. (There's disagreement within the field of peace and conflict studies as to whether vandalism counts as nonviolence.) Trish never diverts from her purpose of stopping this vandalism, but she finds a way to transform the conflict, to move past winners and losers. Or to put it another way, Trish finds a way out of the conflict trap.

Like "For the Snake of Power," "Big Rural" relies on an abridged timeline. In real life, it would probably take a lot more effort to convince a company like Sol Dominion to change their design plans. The same is true for convincing the vandals to stand down. The power company and the local community might go through several rounds of negotiations before arriving at the agro-voltaics plan. With that said, the solution itself is realistic, and it reflects key concepts in conflict transformation theory. Through narrative condensation, Rambo has gotten the essentials across in a compelling short story.

---

[35]Rambo, "Big Rural," 119.

Conclusion

The exploration above hardly exhausts the links between peace studies and peace poetics. By focusing on areas like peace education, civil resistance, and conflict transformation, I've left aside other important areas like restorative justice and post-conflict peacebuilding. On the creative writing side, I've prioritized heroic action over world building in my analysis of the solarpunk stories. (At least world building gets its due in a later chapter.) It wasn't my intention, though, to exhaust every possibility of peace poetics, but merely to offer a proof of concept.

With that said, an action can only happen in a world in which that action is possible. For this reason, before moving on, let's briefly consider crucial elements of world building in these two tales from *Weight of Light* that help facilitate the nonviolent action. Both stories imagine plausible advancements in solar technology, but they don't stop there. Both also pay attention to the social context of technology. Rather than techno-dystopias, these are worlds where leadership must consider the holistic impacts of technology, although it takes pushback from ordinary citizens to insure this consideration.

Furthermore, both stories imagine social structures wherein such pushback can prove effective. Neither story depicts a utopia, of course. In both, powerful corporate or governmental institutions threaten to trample those on the margins. But unlike Orwell's *1984*—which predated Star Trek's Borg in portraying resistance as futile—these societies have space for advocacy, negotiation, and effective resistance. Such narrative worlds allow for nonviolent heroic action.

By reading these stories carefully with an eye toward narrative craft, other writers can pick up ideas for attempting similar effects in their own work. To be clear, I'm not claiming that Cooper and Rambo thought about their work using the same terms I've used. Reading the second half of "For the Snake of Power" as a caper story helps us figure out how to replicate a form of action, whether or not Cooper conceived it that way. Similarly, I don't know if Cat Rambo deliberately drew on conflict transformation theory in "Big Rural," but that field helps us understand why the story's resolution works.

Beyond craft specifics, for civil resistance or conflict transformation to work in fiction, writers must believe that these methods can succeed. That is, writers must craft worlds that allow nonviolent heroism to triumph. Certainly, Cooper and Rambo have done this. If these two stories are any indication, the possibilities for peace poetics are bright.

3

Character Arcs

Characters need coherence. A well-written fictional character will never truly act "out of character." If a character changes, that change should be justified within the narrative. If a character engages in unexpected behavior, that behavior should reveal a new layer to the character. In other words, even apparent contradictions should ultimately expand an audience's understanding of a character. Random shifts for the sake of plot advancement just won't cut it. This general principle also applies to a character's choice of violent or nonviolent means. If you intend for a character to travel a nonviolent path, then you must integrate the potential for nonviolent heroism into the construction and growth arc of that character.

To illustrate this, consider the late wrestling legend Randy Poffo, better known by his ring name Macho Man Randy Savage. Whether as a babyface or heel (hero or villain), his wrestling persona depended upon volatile emotions and outbursts of violence. This was appropriate for his chosen profession, since professional wrestling storytelling is built around heroic violence. Imagine, though, making that same character the main protagonist of a narrative centered on a nonviolent campaign. The character would now be a poor fit for the actions the story required him to take—unless, of course, he went through a transformative growth arc.

This leads to a couple of questions: How do you shape such an arc? And how do you insure that your character is capable of that particular inward journey? This chapter explores one possible approach: incorporating concepts from conflict transformation[1] theory into the character design process. However, since books in that field aren't written for creative writers, I'll also draw links between conflict transformation best-sellers and creative writing handbooks.

We'll start by exploring Lajos Egri's dialectical approach to creative writing from *The Art of Dramatic Writing*. Following that, we'll consider concepts from Adam Kahane's *Power and Love*; K. M. Weiland's *Creating Character Arcs*; and Fisher, Ury, and Patton's *Getting to Yes*. Taken together, these books will help us unpack the potential for conflict transformation and nonviolent action in fictional characters.

Egri's Dialectical Approach

Lajos Egri's *The Art of Dramatic Writing*[2] is one of the most influential creative writing guides of the past century. First published as *How to Write a Play* in 1942, the expanded and retitled edition came out in 1946. It has remained in print ever since.

According to Egri, every work of narrative fiction must have an underlying premise. For example, he gave this as the premise of Shakespeare's *King Lear*: "blind trust leads to destruction."[3] A writer might not always know the premise when they start writing, but they need to find it by the time their work is done. Indeed, a good writer will edit out material extraneous to the premise and revise what remains to support it.[4]

How does an author "prove" their premise, though? By crafting characters who will live that premise out. Egri described a tripartite "bone structure" for fictional characters, made up of

---

[1]Other terms for this field are also common, such as "conflict resolution," "conflict management," and "alternative dispute resolution." Nonetheless, "conflict transformation" seems like the best fit for exploring dynamic character growth. For more on this term, see John Paul Lederach's *The Little Book of Conflict Transformation* (New York: Good Books, 2003).

[2]Lajos Egri, *The Art of Dramatic Writing: Its Basis in the Creative Interpretation of Human Motives* (New York: Simon and Schuster, 1946).

[3]Ibid., 3.

[4]Ibid., 5–6, 9–11.

their physiology, sociology, and psychology. If you understand all dimensions of a fictional character, you can predict how they'll react in a certain situation.[5] But what happens if your character wouldn't believably act in the manner that your premise demands? Then you must tweak the character and/or the situation until the necessary course becomes inevitable—or at the very least, likely.[6]

Let's consider Shakespeare's *King Lear*. In the play, Lear snubs his youngest daughter, Cordelia, and divides the kingdom between her devious sisters, only to have the latter betray him. Lear makes his fateful error early in the play. When deciding how to divide his kingdom, he asks his daughters to declare the extent of their love for him. The elder two are effusive. The eldest, Goneril, says her love for her father is

> Dearer than eyesight, space, and liberty,
> Beyond what can be valued, rich or rare,
> No less than life, with grace, health, beauty, honor

Lear's second daughter, Regan, echoes her sister's sentiments. However, the youngest, Cordelia, refuses to compete with her sisters in this game. She explains that she loves her father to the full extent appropriate for a daughter toward her father. Yet she is expected to marry someday, and thus she will owe a share of love and devotion to her future husband. She cannot honestly echo her sisters' unreserved declarations of love. Lear is insulted by this temperate answer and so favors the flatterers. This leads to his downfall.

If he'd been less rash and more temperate, Lear would never have made such an error. If he'd been a courtier rather than a king, he wouldn't have had the authority to make his great mistake. But Lear's downfall was inevitable, in Shakespeare's play, because he was the right character in the right situation to prove that "blind trust leads to destruction."[7]

---

[5] Ibid., 32–8.

[6] Ibid., 100–6.

[7] William Shakespeare, "King Lear," *The Handy-Volume Shakespeare*, vol. 12 (New York: George Routledge and Sons, *c.* 1910), 5–152. Another powerful character in Shakespeare's play, the Duke of Gloucester, experiences a parallel fall to Lear's. In both cases, the reach of their error corresponds to the scope of their original power.

Not every premise is compatible with nonviolent heroism. If your premise is "ruthless power devours naive idealism," then a nonviolent campaign could hardly be expected to succeed. On the other hand, if your premise is "a just cause overcomes even the greatest odds," then the prospects for nonviolence are much better.

Egri described his method as the dialectical approach to playwriting, based on Hegel's triad of thesis—antithesis—synthesis. The basic idea is that every argument (thesis) provokes a counterargument (antithesis) that leads to a new perspective combining the insights of both (synthesis). Then this synthesis becomes the new thesis, provoking its own antithesis, and finally a new synthesis. And thus it continues. Or to translate that same idea from the realm of rhetoric into the realm of physics: an action (thesis) provokes a reaction (antithesis) that results in a new state (synthesis). But the new state provokes a reaction, so the process continues: an ongoing chain of action and reaction.[8]

Egri believed that this process of action and reaction, when applied to fiction writing, should be rooted in character. The key, according to Egri, is to locate your characters at the point in their lives where they're compelled to act. If the compulsion isn't there, Egri insisted, then you're starting your story in the wrong spot. But if you put the right character in the right situation at the right time, then a dialectical tension—a chain of action and reaction—will drive your story forward.[9]

This dialectical tension can be either internal or external. That is, it can be driven by conflicting forces within a single character, or by conflicts between characters. Egri used the term "unity of opposites" to describe this. Basically, if you get the balance right between the protagonist and antagonist, then their conflict will drive the story forward. (He used the term "orchestration" to describe how characters are balanced against each other overall.)[10] These options aren't exclusive, of course. Internal and external tensions can feed off of each other. Indeed, the notion that you must change yourself in order to change the world is a popular theme in literature, from George Bernard Shaw's *The Devil's Disciple* to Disney's *The Lion King*.

---

[8] Egri, *Dramatic Writing*, 49–50.
[9] Ibid., 182–91.
[10] Ibid., 113–26.

And this synergy is hardly restricted to the field of creative writing. Internal and external change are also interdependent in another dialectically driven field—that of conflict transformation. Indeed, certain concepts from conflict transformation theory can help us think more deeply about the growth arcs of fictional characters, especially characters capable of nonviolent heroism. To explore this further, let's next turn to the titular dyad of Adam Kahane's *Power and Love*.

Writing Exercise #1

The Charles Perrault version of "Little Red Riding Hood" ends with the titular character being eaten by the wolf. (Unlike other versions, Perrault omits the eventual rescue by a woodsman.)

Perrault offers the following moral of the story: "Children, especially attractive, well bred young ladies, should never talk to strangers, for if they should do so, they may well provide dinner for a wolf."[11] To use Egri's terminology, this appears to be the premise of this version of the fairy tale.

a. What is an alternative premise that could lead to a different outcome? Try to come up with a premise that puts Little Red Riding Hood in control of her own fate.

b. What changes would you need to make to Little Red Riding Hood's character for her to live out the new premise?

---

[11]Perrault continues, "I say 'wolf,' but there are various kinds of wolves. There are also those who are charming, quiet, polite, unassuming, complacent, and sweet, who pursue young women at home and in the streets. And unfortunately, it is these gentle wolves who are the most dangerous ones of all." Although not directly applicable to the writing exercise above, Perrault's ironic social commentary is a notable feature of his fairy tales. Original source for the English translation: Andrew Lang, *The Blue Fairy Book* (London, *c.* 1889), 51–3. Charles Perrault, "Little Red Riding Hood," Folklore and Mythology Electronic Texts, https://sites.pitt.edu/~dash/perrault02.html (accessed June 26, 2024).

> c. What character traits might empower Little Red Riding
> Hood to discover a nonviolent solution to the conflict?
> d. What changes would you need to make to the plot of the
> story to suit the updated premise and protagonist?

Based on your answers to the questions above, try to outline or write a story in which Little Red Riding Hood avoids her original tragic fate.

Power and Love

Adam Kahane's *Power and Love* could be described as a hybrid between a conflict transformation manual and a memoir.[12] I'll focus on his core ideas here, rather than the life events that formed them, but Kahane's book is widely available if you wish to explore the latter. Since it comes first in the book title, let's start with Kahane's understanding of power. In brief, power is agency. That is, power is the drive to accomplish one's goals and fulfill one's purpose. As such, power can be a very positive force. Without power, there can be no growth or creativity. Nonetheless, power has a dark side. As Kahane put it, "power to" can morph into "power over." When you're willing to stifle someone else's power—their growth, creativity, and self-actualization—while pursuing your own goals and vision, that's the dark side of power. That's how power turns oppressive and destructive.[13]

If power is the drive toward self-assertion, then love is the drive toward connection. Humans are social animals. Although Darwin honed in on the evolutionary importance of competition, it turns out that cooperation is just as fundamental for our species.[14] When love allows us to create bonds, work toward goals collectively, and champion the growth of not just ourselves but also others, it is

---

[12]Adam Kahane, *Power and Love: A Theory and Practice of Social Change* (San Francisco: Berrett-Koehler Publishers, 2010).
[13]Ibid., 11–27.
[14]Coren L. Apicella and Joan B. Silk, "The Evolution of Human Cooperation," *Current Biology* 29, no. 11 (June 2019), r477–r450.

clearly a force for good. Yet like power, love has a dark side. A person can be so focused on love that they neglect their own needs and wellbeing. A group fixated on everyone getting along might avoid addressing critical issues or making necessary choices. In such situations, love's potential for good fizzles.[15]

Love and power form a potent unity of opposites. But rather than antagonists, they're ultimately dependent upon each other. What keeps power from turning oppressive? An infusion of love. What keeps love from turning impotent? An infusion of power. Neither can be at its best without the other. Kahane argued that we must find a balance of power and love in order to solve the world's most deep-seated problems and conflicts.[16] The same is true for characters tackling problems in fictional worlds.

The dialectical tension between power and love is often strong enough to drive the action in fiction. If we accept this framework, a character arc can move in two directions: toward balance or toward imbalance. The former leads to a happy ending, the latter to tragedy. Let's refer to the former as "comic" to distinguish it from "tragic." We can subdivide further. There are two forms of the comic arc: 1) from a power fixation to balance, or 2) from a love fixation to balance. There are also two forms of the tragic arc: 3) from balance to a power fixation, or 4) from balance to a love fixation. A couple examples will suffice to show that an imbalance in either direction (toward either power or love) can lead to a tragic outcome.

Mob boss Michael Corleone suffers a lonely death at the end of *Godfather III*—a sharp contrast to his father's heart attack while playing with a grandchild (a happy death). Late in the movie, Michael is the target of an assassination attempt. Although he survives, his daughter Mary is killed. This shatters him. The final scene shows Michael Corleone sitting in a garden chair, broken and alone. He slumps, then topples over, apparently dead. A small dog curiously noses his corpse. In the context of the trilogy, this death scene is the final commentary on Michael Corleone's life, decisively marking his arc a tragic one. Kahane's power and love dialectic can shed light on this character's fate. Throughout the *Godfather* films, Michael Corleone reveals the drives toward both power and

---

[15]Kahane, *Power and Love*, 29–50.
[16]Ibid., 26–7, 50, 53–6.

love within him, but power always proves dominant when push comes to shove. Ordering the murder of his own brother at the end of *Godfather II* is the quintessential example of this. Power overwhelms love in the life of Michael Corleone, so he dies alone.[17]

An imbalance toward love can also result in a tragic arc. Consider the kind-hearted protagonist Charlie from the movie *Mean Streets*.[18] Charlie remains stubbornly loyal to his reckless friend Johnny, even after Johnny reneges on a large debt. A devout Catholic, Charlie believes he has a Christian duty to help Johnny. As such, Charlie sticks by his friend despite constant warnings from others. Matters boil over when Johnny mocks and insults his creditor. Ultimately, both Charlie and Johnny are shot and severely injured while trying to escape town. Despite his imbalance toward love, Charlie certainly isn't a weak character. To the contrary, he shows strength by resisting the mounting social pressure to distance himself from Johnny. It isn't weakness but imbalance that leads to Charlie's downfall.

In truth, there are even more permutations to power and love arcs than the four listed above. The original *Godfather* tells the story of how Michael Corleone goes from balance to imbalance. *Godfather III*, however, is the story of how he tries and fails to regain that lost balance. A similar character in another story might succeed. That is, the writer might fit both fall and redemption into a single narrative. On the other hand, Charlie in *Mean Streets* is off-balance toward love from the outset. The tension comes from seeing how long he can last before toppling over. You might come up with other permutations that I've left out, and that's to be encouraged. This treatment of power and love isn't intended as a closed system, but rather as one way to organize our thoughts and stimulate creativity.

Although we considered a couple examples of the tragic arc above, the alternative is actually more important for this book. A protagonist who finds balance, I believe, has a better chance at effective nonviolent heroism than one who loses their balance. As

---

[17]*The Godfather*, directed by Francis Ford Coppola (Paramount Pictures, 1972). *The Godfather: Part II*, directed by Francis Ford Coppola (Paramount Pictures, 1974). *The Godfather: Part III*, directed by Francis Ford Coppola (Paramount Pictures, 1990).

[18]*Mean Streets*, directed by Martin Scorsese (Warner Brothers, 1973).

such, the comic arc deserves a closer look. We'll soon give this arc its due through a detailed example.

First, though, we need a few more concepts from Kahane's book. He conveniently used three movement metaphors for the ways that power and love can relate, which is very useful for helping us think about narrative action. When power and love are completely disconnected from each other, we are in danger of "falling."[19] When they are linked but out of balance, we are prone to "stumbling."[20] And when they are in "dynamic balance," we are capable of "walking." As Kahane pointed out, when we walk, we don't actually move our legs in unison. That would be hopping. Rather, we constantly and fluidly alternate between our legs (another dialectical process, one could argue).[21] In fiction with a comic arc, the triumphant protagonist should achieve a similar "dynamic balance" between power and love. Using Kahane's metaphors, the two arcs are as follows:

> Tragic arc: walking → stumbling → falling
> Comic arc: falling → stumbling → walking

Now let's look closely at an example of the latter.

Case Study: *Trading Places*

To see the dialectic of power and love in action, consider Louis Winthorpe III (played by Dan Aykroyd) from the 1983 comedy *Trading Places*.[22] At the beginning of the film, Louis is the managing director of Duke & Duke Commodities Brokers, owned by Randolf and Mortimer Duke. After a run-in with Billy Ray Valentine, a street hustler played by Eddie Murphy, the Duke brothers decide to make Louis and Billy Ray the subjects of an elaborate bet/social experiment—is "nature" or "nurture" more responsible for the differences between the commodities broker and the hustler?

---

[19]Kahane, *Power and Love*, 57–73.
[20]Ibid., 75–102.
[21]Ibid., 54, 103–26.
[22]*Trading Places*, directed by John Landis (Paramount Pictures, 1983).

To find out, the Duke brothers frame Louis for embezzlement and drug dealing. As a result, his bank accounts are frozen, he's barred from his company-owned home, his fiancé leaves him, and all his friends abandon him. For the other half of their experiment, the Duke brothers install Billy Ray as the replacement for Louis. The latter is as baffled by his rise in life as the former is by his downfall.

But why is Louis susceptible to such a dramatic fall? Because, to use Kahane's terminology, his love and power are disconnected. In fact, he's entirely unbalanced toward power at the beginning of the movie. This serves him well as a Wall Street "master of the universe." But when the Duke brothers play their prank, none of Louis's personal connections stand by him, not even his fiancé. His closest relationships prove superficial.

What eventually saves Louis is the establishment of new personal ties, first with a prostitute named Ophelia who takes him in after his fall, and later with Billy Ray himself. The latter learns that his rise was due to a cruel bet, and furthermore overhears the Duke brothers plotting to kick both him and Louis to the curb. Billy Ray reaches out to Louis, and together they come up with a scheme to take revenge on the Duke brothers. In the process, the two men become friends.

Using Kahane's framework, the character arc of Louis Winthorpe III could be summarized thus: he initially "falls" when his power and love are disconnected. Then he "stumbles" as he begins reconnecting with love, but remains fixated on power. Finally he "walks" at the end of the movie, when his return to power is balanced and supported by his relationships with Olivia and Billy Ray.

Trading Places also illustrates Egri's concepts of "orchestration" and "unity of opposites." The initial "unity of opposites" is between Louis and Billy Ray. The screenwriters, however, leave room for their eventual alliance through a clever mechanism—they have the Duke brothers act as "dramatists" in the first half of the movie. It is the Duke brothers, after all, who "orchestrate" the conflict between Louis and Billy Ray, who entwine the fates of these antagonists so that one must fall for the other to rise.

Unlike the movie's screenwriters, though, the Duke brothers live in the same universe as their morality play's "characters," which allows Louis and Billy Ray to both discover and rebel against the narrative into which the Dukes have cast them. At this point, the true "unity of opposites" emerges: Louis and Billy Ray vs. Randolf and Mortimer Duke. There's even a parallel to the conflict dynamic from the Dukes' social experiment; one of these pairs must fall for the other to rise. The orchestration in *Trading Places* is masterful.

Admittedly, *Trading Places* doesn't have anything to say about the power of nonviolence—certainly not directly so. Nonetheless, it is an unexpectedly relevant example. In the next chapter I'll argue that the caper story genre, where the protagonists attempt a heist or con, offers a valuable structural model for stories with nonviolent campaigns. In addition to being a screwball comedy, *Trading Places* is also a caper story. Louis and Billy Ray get their revenge by orchestrating a "con" on the Dukes. It's a good sign, therefore, that these conflict transformation concepts fit so well with the film's central character arc. But we still have more to explore on the topic of character arcs, so further discussion of capers and campaigns must wait.

Writing Exercise #2

Imagine a character who is a community organizer in a city with extreme economic inequality. They're trying to bring pressure on the city leaders to raise the minimum wage and invest in affordable housing. This character is fixated on power, and the lie they believe is as follows: the ends justify the means. Based on this character, sketch out answers to the following questions.

   a. What does this character want most?
   b. What is the truth they need to learn?
   c. Were this character fixated on love instead of power, what would their lie and truth be?
   d. What would they want and need?
   e. For both versions, what does their fall look like? What does stumbling look like? What does walking look like?

Using your answers to the questions above, you could sketch out either a "power → balance" or "love → balance" story. Which do you find more promising, and why? Perhaps try this exercise again with different initial scenarios. Hopefully, you'll find an option that you want to write about.

Creating Character Arcs

Although Kahane's ideas have proven very useful, conflict transformation theory is hardly the only place to find dialectical pairings that drive character arcs in fiction. Indeed, writers since Egri have come up with their own ways of analyzing characters. For example, the novelist K. M. Weiland offered a pair of intertwined dyads—"the truth vs. the lie" and "wants vs. needs"—in her 2016 book *Creating Character Arcs*.[23] Although Weiland didn't describe her approach as dialectical, or even draw on Egri explicitly, she's a good example of how his concept of the "unity of opposites" continues to exert at least an indirect influence on American writers.

In *Creating Character Arcs*, Weiland built on earlier ideas that first surfaced in the film industry (one of the spaces where Egri proved most influential). According to David Bordwell in his 2006 book *The Way Hollywood Tells It*, "Screenplay manuals occasionally distinguish between what the character wants (the external goal) and what the character needs (the underlying motivation, driven by flaws and ghosts). ... Given a flaw, the character must conquer it. Hence, the character arc."[24] A decade later, these concepts would form the core of Weiland's *Creating Character Arcs*. Weiland, however, took these concepts out of Hollywood and made them accessible to fiction writers across genres.

Over half of Weiland's book focuses on what she calls the positive change arc (as opposed to the flat arc or the negative change arc).

---

[23]K. M. Weiland, *Creating Character Arcs: The Masterful Author's Guide to Uniting Story Structure, Plot, and Character Development* (South Yorkshire, UK: PenForASword Publishing, 2016).
[24]David Bordwell, *The Way Hollywood Tells It: Story and Style in Modern Movies* (Berkeley, CA: University of California Press, 2006), 29–30.

In order for the protagonist to experience a positive change over the course of the story, there must be something wrong with them at the beginning. However, they may not know this, or may be mistaken about what is wrong. That's because the protagonist's true problems are rooted in the lie they believe. The arc of the story, though, leads them toward the truth they need to learn.[25]

Charles Dickens' *A Christmas Carol* provides a classic example of this. At the beginning of the story, the miserly Ebeneezer Scrooge believes a powerful lie: charity and compassion are weaknesses, for personal gain is the only thing that matters. This is made apparent early in the book when a pair of gentlemen show up at Scrooge's office. They are taking up a collection for the poor. Scrooge refuses to contribute, though, and suggests that the poor should instead be put into prisons or workhouses.

Later in the book, Scrooge encounters three holiday spirits: the Ghosts of Christmas Present, Past, and Yet to Come. At one point, the Ghost of Christmas Present reveals a pair of impoverished children clutching his robe. These prove to be allegorical representations of Ignorance and Want. The spirit warns that if their needs aren't alleviated, the pair will prove the doom of humankind. Scrooge asks, "Have they no refuge or resource?" But the spirit mocks Scrooge with his own unkind words. "Are there no Prisons? ... Are there no workhouses?" Scrooge's concern for the children suggests that his transformation has already begun, but it will take more revelations for the miser to fully change. By the end of the story, thanks to his adventures with the Christmas ghosts, Scrooge learns this essential truth: what make life meaningful are human connections and caring for others.[26]

We have, then, a dialectical tension between the truth and the lie: two opposing forces within a character, a unity of opposites. If a story follows Weiland's arc, then the truth must ultimately outlast the lie.

Although the positive change arc is essentially a comic arc, it's worth noting that Aristotle's conception of tragedy included a similar transition. According to Aristotle, the tragic hero must

---

[25]Weiland, *Character Arcs*, 25–35.

[26]Charles Dickens, *A Christmas Carol* (New York: Weathervane Books, 1977). Weiland offered a slightly different phrasing of Scrooge's lie: "a man's worth can only be measured by the amount of money he has earned" (*Character Arcs*, 28).

face a moment of recognition in which their false understanding is stripped away and the terrible truth becomes clear. Aristotle's favorite example of this was Sophocles' play *Oedipus the King*. Oedipus discovers that he has unwittingly killed his biological father and married his biological mother—a moment of damning clarity that leads him to gouge out his eyes.[27] However, in Weiland's positive change arc, contra Aristotelian tragedy, embracing the truth leads to redemption, not doom.

Closely related to "the lie vs. the truth" is another dichotomy, "wants vs. needs." What the protagonist wants at the beginning of the story might be a good thing or a bad thing, but it isn't the essential thing. It isn't what they character needs most. Instead, what they really need is to reject the lie and embrace the truth. Depending on the story, satisfying the need may either be a prerequisite or a substitute for satisfying their want.[28]

Consider the movie *Cars*, one of Weiland's go-to examples. Throughout the film, the race car Lightning McQueen wants to win the Piston Cup and secure a premier sponsorship. At the end of the movie, though, he gives up both of these things. He helps another car finish the race, thus sacrificing his own chance to win, and he even turns down the desired sponsorship. He does these things because he realizes that relationships are more important than individual success. Learning that lesson, of course, is what he truly needs to grow as a person.[29] (He's not a human, but he is a person in the context of the film.[30])

In the movie *Crazy Rich Asians*, conversely, the protagonist Rachel Chu wants to marry Nick, her wealthy boyfriend, and they indeed end up happily engaged.[31] This only happens, though, after

---

[27]Aristotle, *Poetics*, book 11. S. H. Butcher, *Aristotle's Theory of Poetry and Fine Art: With a Critical Text and Translation of the Poetics*, 4th ed. with corrections (London: Macmillan and Co., 1911), 41.

[28]Weiland, *Character Arcs*, 33–8.

[29]*Cars*, directed by John Lasseter and Joe Ranft (Pixar, 2006). Weiland, *Character Arcs*, 37.

[30]I'm hardly the first creative writing theorist to make such a distinction. Janet Burroway makes a similar point regarding Bugs Bunny and several other fictional rabbits in *Writing Fiction: A Guide to Narrative Craft*, 10th ed. (Chicago: University of Chicago, 2019), 44.

[31]*Crazy Rich Asians*, directed by Jon M. Chu (Warner Brothers, 2018).

difficult experiences with Nick's snobby family lead her to reject his first proposal. Nick is ready to turn his back on his family over the mistreatment of the woman he loves. However, Rachel understands that this is too high a price for him to pay, and it would establish a shaky foundation for their future happiness. She rejects Nick's proposal because she has learned that her self-respect matters more than being with any man. What she needs, more than she needs Nick, is to embrace this truth. By doing so, though, she finally earns the respect of Nick's mother, which leads to the happy ending. (The ring used in Nick's second proposal is a family heirloom that he could only have obtained from his mother. This signifies her acceptance of Rachel as a worthy match.) This is a good example of how a protagonist might still obtain the thing they want, but only after they realize that they don't fundamentally need it.

If we look at the last two examples above, it's clear that we can also analyze them in terms of love and power. Lightning McQueen is fixated on power at the beginning of *Cars*, but he learns to bring love into the picture. Conversely, Rachel Chu is focused on love at the beginning of *Crazy Rich Asians*. But by insisting on her own self-worth, even at the cost of her engagement, she reconnects to her power.

The trick to harmonizing Kahane and Weiland is this: the truth in a story will be related to whichever half of power and love is initially neglected, and the lie will be related to whichever one is initially emphasized. Consider again Scrooge's arc in *A Christmas Carol*:

The lie: Personal gain is the only thing that matters. (Power)
The truth: What makes life meaningful is caring for others. (Love)

Scrooge is initially imbalanced toward power and away from love; his lie and truth reflect this.

Clearly we can weave Kahane's conflict transformation concepts into the character design process. If that is so, then we should certainly be able to create characters capable of handling conflict nonviolently—or perhaps I should say, characters capable of learning alternatives to violence. This doesn't mean writing stories without conflict; it just means that different tactics and resolutions are possible. Nor is Kahane the only theorist whose work can be repurposed in this manner. In fact, one of the most influential negotiation texts of the past half century, *Getting to Yes*, resonates with Weiland in intriguing ways. Let's turn to that next.

Getting to Yes

Roger Fisher and William Ury's conflict transformation classic, *Getting to Yes*, was first published in 1983. (Bruce Patton has been credited as a co-author since the 1991 second edition.) A key concept of *Getting to Yes* is the distinction between interests and positions. A position is what someone is asking for, or even demanding, in a dispute. An interest is what they actually *need* or *desire*.[32] This dichotomy is now one of the most influential concepts in conflict transformation theory, appearing in later works like Jacqueline M. Nolan-Haley's *Alternative Dispute Resolution in a Nutshell* and Christopher W. Moore's *The Mediation Process*, to give just two examples.[33]

Fisher, Ury, and Patton offer an interesting example of this dichotomy. They ask us to imagine two children fighting over the last orange in the fridge. Their mother solves this dispute by slicing the orange down the middle. Each child gets one half, a perfectly just solution. Afterwards, the first child throws the orange peel away, then puts the pulp into a juicer. The second child throws the pulp away, then grates up the orange peel to use in a pie crust. As it turns out, the two children wanted different parts of the orange. Unfortunately, they were focused on their positions ("I must have the orange!" "No, I must have the orange!") instead of their interests (making orange juice vs. making a pie). Because of this, the family failed to reach the wisest solution—giving one child the pulp and the other the peel.[34]

---

[32]Roger Fisher, William Ury, and Bruce Patton, *Getting to Yes: Negotiating Agreement Without Giving In*, 3rd ed. (New York: Penguin Books, 2011), 42–57.

[33]Jacqueline M. Nolan-Haley, *Alternative Dispute Resolution in a Nutshell*, 4th ed. (Saint Paul, MN: West Academic, 2013), 25–31, 79. Christopher W. Moore, *The Mediation Process: Practical Strategies for Resolving Conflict*, 4th ed. (San Francisco, CA: Jossey-Bass, 2014), 171–8, 291–7, 395–400.

[34]Fisher, Ury, and Patton, *Getting to Yes*, 58–9. I offer above an embellished version of the tale.

Obviously, not all disputes can be settled in so tidy a manner, but the notion of a "wise agreement" is still very useful. *Getting to Yes* offers this definition of that concept: "A wise agreement ... meets the legitimate interests of each side to the extent possible, resolves conflicting interests fairly, is durable, and takes community interests into account."[35]

Now, if characters in conflict reach a wise agreement right away, that's not much of a story. The process of moving from one stance to another, though, has great narrative potential. In the earlier stages of a story, antagonists may be locked in an adversarial struggle rooted in incompatible positions. By the end, though, to use the language of Fisher and Ury, they might learn to "focus on interests, not positions" and "invent options for mutual gain."[36] For this transformation to truly be compelling, though, it should synchronize with the growth arcs of major characters—especially that of the protagonist. For that reason, it's worthwhile to map the dyad of "interests vs. positions" onto the two dyads from *Creating Character Arcs*. There are actually two ways to do this.

Let's start with the more obvious approach. First, we need to cluster the related character arc concepts together. As noted above, the truth is connected to what a person actually needs. Conversely, the want is often (but not always) linked to or rooted in the lie. Thus, we can pair the concepts up as follows: lie/wants and truth/needs. The next question, then, is what do we do with interests and positions? Well, according to *Getting to Yes*, our interests are what are most essential, and getting locked into a position may actually get in the way of pursuing our interests. In other words, there's a resonance between the lie/wants and positions, and a similar resonance between the truth/needs and interests. Or to put it concisely:

lie/wants ≈ positions
truth/needs ≈ interests[37]

---

[35]Ibid., 4.

[36]Ibid., 13.

[37]I'm using the double-tilde wavy equals sign to indicate a strong resonance between these concepts, rather than an exact equivalence. I realize that this isn't quite how the symbol is used in physics or engineering, but since the topic at hand is poetics, I'm exercising poetic license.

Consider again the plot arc I proposed above, where antagonists go from being locked in a struggle over incompatible positions to finding a wise solution based on their actual interests. We can easily bring the character arc concepts into this. At the beginning, the characters believe the lie: namely, that sticking firm to their positions is the only way to get what they want. Ultimately, though, they must discover the truth: by focusing on their underlying interests they can find an alternative solution that gets them what they need.

We see this dynamic play out in Julia Quinn's novel *The Duke and I* (or if you prefer, the first season of *Bridgerton*).[38] Daphne Bridgerton wants to get married and have a large family, like the loving one she grew up in. Simon Hastings, who never knew his mother and hated his father, has sworn never to marry or have children. They fall in love of course.

At first, Daphne and Simon try to find a midway point between their positions. They'll get married but won't have children. It helps that Daphne thinks her husband is sterile. Having received a painfully inadequate sex education from her mother, Daphne doesn't initially grasp the significance of her husband "pulling out." She is merely naive, though, not stupid. Once she figures things out, it leads to a breach in the marriage.

Daphne seduces her husband in his sleep, an impulsive act that leaves Simon feeling panicked and betrayed. His childhood stutter returns—the source of his father's rejection. Barely able to speak, Simon flees the room. Then he flees the mansion as well, retreating to another one of his estates.

For the relationship to heal, Simon has to complete his growth arc. His position that he must never reproduce is rooted in his want, to take revenge on his dead father, and his belief in a powerful lie: that ending his family line is the best way to take that revenge. His greatest interest, though, is to live a full and happy life. To do this, he needs to embrace the truth that living well is actually the best revenge. When Simon is finally ready to step out from the shadow cast by his father's ghost, he's able to reconcile with Daphne, and they start a family together.

You may be thinking, of course they work things out, it's a romance novel! But let's not overlook that Quinn's novel features

---

[38]Julia Quinn, *The Duke and I* (New York: HarperCollins, 2000).

compelling conflict, and it's driven by characters who resolve that conflict nonviolently. Their romance is arguably a successful negotiation. These conflict transformation concepts help us understand why.

There's also another way to link the concepts from *Getting to Yes* with those from *Creating Character Arcs*. This one is less intuitive. On the one hand, a character's "wants" and "needs" are both things that a character might try to obtain. These things could be either abstract or concrete, but they are hypothetically obtainable: dignity, the Maltese Falcon, a job promotion, etc. On the other hand, "the truth" and "the lie" both reflect beliefs and attitudes about those things that a character is trying to obtain. The truth may reflect the right beliefs and attitudes, and the lie the wrong ones, but we're dealing with beliefs and attitudes either way. In a negotiation, your interests don't actually have to reflect deep-seated needs. They could, in fact, simply be whatever you want from the situation. Viewed from this angle, "interests" pairs with both "wants" and "needs." As for your position, it reflects what you believe about your interests. Since the lie and the truth reflect what you believe about your wants and needs, "position" could pair with both "lie" and "truth." In other words:

Things to obtain: interests, wants, needs
Beliefs about things to obtain: positions, lie, truth

Or to revise those earlier equations:

wants, needs ≈ interests
lie, truth ≈ positions

I realize that it may seem contradictory to have two different ways of arranging these sets of concepts. Try thinking of these different arrangements as alternative tools in your writing toolbox. Each one is useful for different tasks. This second framework can help make the three-dimensionality of fictional characters pop. Their positions may reflect a tangled jumble of lies and truths. Only by separating these out can characters advocate for what's most important. Their interests may likewise prove a mish-mash of wants and needs. They must learn to prioritize these, or their energies will be misspent. If we understand these entanglements, then we can decipher the pattern of a particular character's contradictions. Those contradictions create the complexity that bring fictional characters to life.

Lajos Egri also appreciated the significance of character contradiction. He dedicated an entire chapter to this topic in *The Art of Creative Writing*, the sequel to *The Art of Dramatic Writing*. Using his dialectical process, he pitted the following thesis and antithesis against each other: "people change" vs. "people don't change." Egri ultimately concluded that change results from people applying different strategies to satisfy the same underlying need: the need to be important.[39]

While I think Egri's analysis has merit, I don't think the sole concept of "importance" allows for as fine-grained an analysis as the six concepts we've just explored: lie, truth, wants, needs, interests, positions. If we understand how these affect our characters, then we can determine how those characters might unknot themselves—or to switch metaphors, how they might find routes out of their particular dark woods. Sometimes characters are doomed to tragedy because their authors can't find alternate paths for them. These conflict transformation concepts can help us figure out those alternatives.

Writing Exercise #3

Imagine a pair of adult siblings fighting for control of the family grocery business. One sibling is pushing an initiative to bring affordable produce into food deserts. The other wants to pursue grocery delivery services in affluent areas. They are locked in a conflict over which new initiative to invest in. Based on these characters, sketch out answers to the following questions.

   a. What lies might be influencing each character's initial position?
   b. What interests do they have in common?

---

[39]Lajos Egri, *The Art of Creative Writing* (New York: Citadel Press, 1995), 56–69.

> c. What obstacles are interfering with them finding that common ground? How are these obstacles connected to each character's lie?
> d. What truth do these characters need to learn before they can find common ground?
> e. What wise solution might be possible once they grasp that truth?
> f. What are each character's wants and needs? How do they learn to prioritize them wisely?

Now invent your own pair of characters in conflict, and answer these questions for them. Keeping in mind Egri's concept of the "unity of opposites," make sure your characters are well matched for driving forward a high-stakes conflict.

Conclusion

Egri argued that dialectical tensions—tensions between characters or within a character—must drive the plot forward. After drawing on both conflict transformation and writing craft books, we now have a handful of dialectical pairs to play with: power and love, the truth and the lie, wants and needs, positions and interests. These dyads can be creatively combined to help us craft characters who are able to find alternatives to violence. Nonetheless, not every way of linking these concepts together will suit every story. My goal hasn't been to create an airtight system. (As a writer, I find that airtight systems stifle creativity.) Rather, think of these concepts and their various combinations as tools to pull from your writing toolbox as needed.

Furthermore, this exploration is a good starting point, but it hardly exhausts the ways that creative writing and conflict transformation texts might speak to each other. To give just a couple other possibilities:

(1) You could compare the treatment of emotions in *The Emotional Craft of Fiction: How to Write a Story Beneath the*

Surface by Donald Maass and *Beyond Reason: Using Emotions as You Negotiate* by Roger Fisher and Daniel Shapiro.[40]
OR
(2) You could keep Jacqueline M. Nolan Haley's *Alternative Dispute Resolution in a Nutshell* on your desk while writing a legal thriller. (I haven't found a dedicated book on writing legal thrillers, but there are several good articles on the topic.)[41]

No doubt other pairings offer their own creative synergies. Although the process requires a bit of thinking and experimentation, by repurposing conflict transformation concepts we gain additional tools for our writer's toolbox. Most importantly, for the purpose of this book, these new tools can help us craft characters who believably engage in nonviolent heroism.

---

[40]Donald Maass, *The Emotional Craft of Fiction: How to Write the Story Beneath the Surface* (Cincinnati, OH: Writer's Digest Books, 2016). Roger Fisher and Daniel Shapiro, *Beyond Reason: Using Emotions as You Negotiate* (New York: Penguin Books, 2005).

[41]For example: Michael H. Rubin, "Five Tips for Writing a Compelling Legal Thriller," *Strand Magazine*, August 24, 2017, https://strandmag.com/five-tips-writing-compelling-legal-thriller/ (accessed September 24, 2024). Craig Pittman, "How to Write Legal Thrillers that Won't Drive Lawyers Crazy with Mistakes and Inventions," *CrimeReads*, June 19, 2020, https://crimereads.com/how-to-write-legal-thrillers-that-wont-drive-lawyers-crazy-with-mistakes-and-inventions/ (accessed September 24, 2024).

4

Campaigns

Campaigns are sequences of actions that seek to accomplish particular goals. The English word "campaign" originally referred to open countryside (from a French word of the same meaning), and then was extended to military operations across such countryside. This latter meaning eventually superseded the original and was transferred to other types of operations.[1] The military campaign has provided the spine for powerful literary works from the *Iliad* to *Saving Private Ryan*. Political campaigns can also support entertaining narratives, as movies like *The Candidate* and *Election* show. So can courtroom dramas, which feature "campaigns" to win acquittal or conviction. Harper Lee's *To Kill a Mockingbird*, which won the Pulitzer Prize in 1961, is an outstanding example of this genre.

In romantic comedies, violence is an optional element, as the primary campaign is to win someone's heart. Take Shakespeare's *As You Like It*, for example. Although the hero Orlando engages in occasional violent heroics, they aren't the focus of the play. The villainous Duke Frederick isn't overthrown, but instead voluntarily abdicates following an offstage religious conversion.[2] While the story's political resolution is simplistic, its romantic resolution (driven by the heroine Rosalind's clever machinations) is quite elaborate. Shakespeare understood that he was writing a romantic

---

[1] "campaign, n." *Oxford English Dictionary*, OED Online (Oxford University Press), https://doi.org/10.1093/OED/1126270477 (accessed December 2023).
[2] William Shakespeare, "As You Like It," *The Handy-Volume Shakespeare*, vol. 4 (New York: George Routledge and Sons, *c.* 1910), 5–114.

comedy with a political backdrop, not a political drama with a romantic subplot. In other popular romantic comedies, such as the 1980s classic *When Harry Met Sally* or Disney Channel's *High School Musical*, violence is even further sidelined.

Nonviolent campaigns, though, are different from this. These are not campaigns for which violence is irrelevant, but rather they represent an intentional choice of alternative means. Biopics like *Gandhi* and *Selma* provide clear examples of such campaigns, and they remind us that nonviolence can prove effective in the real world. However, violent heroism isn't restricted to the genre of historical drama, so nonviolent heroism shouldn't be either.

Military campaigns, political campaigns, courtroom showdowns, romantic pursuits—these all occur in real life. What shows up on the fictional page, though, is far from a precise transcript of daily living. Even realistic fiction must edit and organize its material into a satisfying narrative arc. Furthermore, a strong enough narrative can lead us to embrace unrealistic and impossible elements, like talking dragons or muscle cars that leap between skyscrapers. The same principle applies to nonviolent campaigns in fiction. It isn't enough to understand how nonviolent campaigns work. (There are plenty of resources for that, after all.) We have to find the right plot beats to give such campaigns a satisfying narrative shape. For that, I recommend we look in an unexpected place: the caper story.

What Is a Caper Story?

The caper story is a subgenre of crime fiction and a cousin of the more famous detective story. The caper story reverses the arrow of the detective story, though. In the latter, the crime has already happened. The detective identifies the criminal and decodes how they pulled off their crime. On the other hand, the caper story watches a scheme unfold. The tension and intrigue come from wondering whether the protagonist will pull off their crime and how.

Technically, there are a cluster of crime fiction subgenres that do this: the confidence tale, the caper story, the heist film. However, in his book *Crime Thriller*, Paul Tomlinson treats both "cons" and "heists" as subcategories of "capers."[3] They both involve criminals enacting a scheme—either an elaborate scam or an elaborate robbery—and both invert the structure of the detective story. Since we're repurposing these structural bones for stories featuring nonviolent campaigns, the similarities between heist and confidence tales matter more than their differences. For that reason, I'm following Tomlinson in using "caper story" as an umbrella term for all of these subgenres.

Like the detective story, the caper story has its roots in the nineteenth century. Writers like Herman Melville, Louisa May Alcott, and Edgar Allen Poe all wrote about characters who sought to swindle their victims.[4] Poe, notably, is also credited with inventing the detective story (although stories with similar features can be found in earlier literature). Also like detective stories, tales featuring cons and heists—such as W. R. Burnett's 1949 heist novel *The Asphalt Jungle*—took on a more hard-boiled quality in the first half of the twentieth century. Eventually, popular films like *The Asphalt Jungle* (adapted from the novel), *The Sting*, and *Ocean's Eleven* brought cons and heists to the silver screen.

Can we really take the caper story structure outside of the crime fiction genre to use for a different purpose, though? Not only can we, but examples already exist. Although not technically part of the confidence tale genre, the trickster tales that pop up in mythology and folklore around the world often have schemes and plot beats similar to those found in confidence tales. In fact, Warwick Wadlington drew heavily on the trickster archetype in his book *The Confidence Game in American Literature*.[5]

We should also consider the biblical *Book of Esther*, in which Queen Esther and her uncle Mordecai carry out a clever scheme to defeat the villainous vizier Haman, thereby saving the Jewish

---

[3]Paul Tomlinson, *Crime Thriller: How to Write Detective, Noir, Caper & Heist, Gangster, & Police Procedurals* (independently published, 2019), 210.

[4]Gary Lindberg, *The Confidence Man in American Literature* (New York: Oxford University Press, 1982). Gail K. Smith, "Who Was That Masked Woman?: Gender and Form in Louisa May Alcott's Confidence Stories," in *American Women Short Story Writers: A Collection of Critical Essays*, ed. Julie Brown (New York: Garland Publishing, 1995), 45–59.

[5]Warwick Wadlington, *The Confidence Game in American Literature* (Princeton, NJ: Princeton University Press, 1975), 5–23.

people. Their scheme has the structure of a "con," even though the story clearly isn't crime fiction. Rather, this would likely have been classified as a sage tale when it was created, like the ones found in the *Book of Daniel*. (The Septuagint version of *Daniel*, which Roman Catholic and Eastern Orthodox Christians treat as canonical, also includes a "detective story" in "Susanna and the Elders." However, this would also have been considered a sage tale in its day.)[6]

A more recent example would be P. G. Wodehouse's Jeeves tales. In these stories, the supremely intelligent valet Jeeves must repeatedly come up with clever schemes to extract his employer, Bernie Wooster, from trouble. Usually, Bernie first gets himself into that trouble with a not-so-clever scheme of his own.[7] These tales fall within the comedy of manners genre, but their structure is close to that of a caper story. The examples of Wodehouse and *Esther* show that it is possible to repurpose the caper story form for use outside of crime fiction.

Underdogs vs. Powerful Figure or Force

Before looking more closely at the structure of caper stories, let's consider a useful parallel between real world nonviolent heroism and how caper stories handle their protagonists. Nonviolent campaigns are generally waged against powerful and oppressive figures or forces. Over the past half century, this dynamic has also made its way into caper stories.

The protagonist of the classic confidence tale is a grifter, someone who makes their way through life by swindling others. In a heist story, the protagonist is often a clever thief who steals from others, but with an intellectual component. Either way, that figure is more antihero than hero. This can render the protagonist unsympathetic, which in turn can hurt the appeal of the story. The classic way to deal with this dilemma is by making the victim complicit in their

---

[6]*The New Oxford Annotated Bible (New Revised Standard Version)*, 5th ed. (New York: Oxford University Press, 2018).
[7]P. G. Wodehouse, *Carry On, Jeeves* (New York: Penguin Books, 1956).

victimhood. As linguistics professor David Maurer explained in his 1940 study *The Big Con*, "the fundamental dishonesty of his victim" is an essential ingredient for many scams.[8]

The earliest American confidence tales relied on this basic dynamic: the victims were made vulnerable by their own greed or bad impulses. The same is also true of certain contemporary scams. The "Nigerian prince" emails that circulated several years back depended on their prospective targets' willingness to launder money.[9] The "greedy mark" dynamic doesn't directly apply to heists, but in hard-boiled worlds like those of classic pulp fiction or Frank Miller's *Sin City* comics, the notion that "no one is innocent" is almost atmospheric. This helps bring crime victims down to the level of criminal protagonists, making it easier for readers to lean into their identification with the criminals.

There may be a limit, though, to an audience's willingness to accept that "no one is innocent." After all, there are many real world fraud victims who shouldn't be treated as meaningfully complicit in their own victimhood. Consider, for example, the rank and file Enron employees who were encouraged to invest their retirement funds in company stock at the same time that the top executives were secretly divesting theirs.[10] Investing in the company you work for and failing to sufficiently diversify your retirement portfolio is hardly comparable to betting on a rigged fight or engaging in an embezzlement scheme.

Or consider this, many contemporary phone scammers deliberately prey on the elderly, who may be suffering from Alzheimer's disease or dementia. Mauro V. Corvasce and Joseph R. Paglino warned about such scams in *Modus Operandi*, but the rise of robocalls since that book came out has automated the process of

---

[8]David Maurer, *The Big Con: The Story of the Confidence Man* (New York: MJF Books, 1999), 2.

[9]To be clear, this type of scam is hardly unique to Nigeria, and online scammers can easily misrepresent their nationalities. Advance-fee scams have been around for centuries and pop up in all corners of the world.

[10]Some of these employees were interviewed in the documentary *Enron: The Smartest Guys in the Room*, directed by Alex Gibney (Jigsaw Productions, 2005). See also: Bethany McLean and Peter Elkind, *The Smartest Guys in the Room: The Amazing Rise and Scandalous Fall of Enron*, 10th anniversary ed. (New York: Penguin Books, 2013). Kurt Eichenwald, *Conspiracy of Fools: A True Story* (New York: Broadway Books, 2005).

finding potential victims.[11] Both CNN and Fox Business News have reported on elderly victims committing suicide after losing their life savings to such scams.[12] Given the tragic cost of these real world crimes, audiences may require a more compelling reason to root for fictional criminals.

The 1973 film *The Sting* strikes on a better solution to this issue by making the antagonist a dangerous mob boss, allowing the protagonists to look heroic in comparison. The 2003 film *Confidence* copies this device. In both films, a team of grifters unwittingly swindle an agent of a major crime boss. In both cases, the crime boss puts out a hit on them, leading to the death of one of the con artists. The survivors decide to take their revenge by running a major scam on the crime boss. This creates an underdog dynamic for the con artists, making it easy to root for them.

The same solution works in heist films. In the 2001 *Ocean's Eleven* remake starring George Clooney, the crime boss figure is replaced by the powerful and Machiavellian casino owner Terry Benedict, played by Andy Garcia.[13] Admittedly, Benedict's main claims to villainy are dating Danny Ocean's ex-wife and being violently opposed to having his casinos robbed. Typed out in print like that, it's not entirely obvious why he should be the villain. Thanks to the performances of Clooney and Garcia, though, the film successfully sells the "David vs. Goliath" dynamic to the audience.

The TV show *Leverage* invests completely in this underdog dynamic, making it central to the show's premise.[14] In *Leverage*, a former insurance investigator leads a team of criminals: a grifter, a thief, a hacker, the muscle. This team pulls off a new con or heist each episode. Much like the A-Team, though, the *Leverage* team only uses its skills to help those oppressed by wealthy and powerful

---

[11]Mauro V. Corvasce and Joseph R. Paglino, *Modus Operandi: A Writer's Guide to How Criminals Work* (Cincinnati OH: Writer's Digest Books, 1995), 71–3.

[12]Wayne Drash, "Driven to Death by Phone Scammers," CNN, October 7, 2015, https://www.cnn.com/2015/10/07/us/jamaica-lottery-scam-suicide/index.html. "Elderly Robocall Scam Victim Committed Suicide after 'Fraudsters' Stole Life Savings," Fox Business, July 17, 2019, https://www.foxbusiness.com/features/robocall-scam-victim-suicide-stole-life-saving (both accessed September 23, 2024).

[13]*Ocean's Eleven*, directed by Steven Soderbergh (Warner Brothers, 2001).

[14]*Leverage*, created by Chris Downey and John Rogers (Electric Entertainment, 2008–12).

villains. With *Leverage*, then, the caper story effectively circles back around to the old Robin Hood legends.

This underdog dynamic translates quite well to stories that feature nonviolent campaigns. Think of Gandhi versus the British Raj, or the Civil Rights Movement versus Jim Crow. Both have that David versus Goliath vibe—the underdog facing off against the powerful figure or force. Not only that, but unlike the grifter antihero, the nonviolent protagonist can be presented as unproblematically heroic (though you can also introduce rough edges to make the character more interesting). In other words, the caper story genre has developed in a direction that 1) makes caper story protagonists more sympathetic, and 2) makes it easier (or more intuitive) to map nonviolent heroism onto the bones of the caper story's narrative structure.

The movie *Selma*—based on the famous 1965 civil rights march from Selma to Montgomery, Alabama—is a good example of pairing the underdog dynamic with nonviolent heroism.[15] The film depicts the oppression of African-Americans in Alabama during the 1960s. This includes being denied their constitutional voting rights. Activists like Martin Luther King, Jr. must challenge the forces of white supremacy—personified in the film by the racist local sheriff, Jim Clark; violent to the point of murderous law enforcement officers; and the arch-segregationist Governor of Alabama, George Wallace. Meanwhile, potential allies like President Lyndon Johnson worry that the push for a Voting Rights Act, coming so close on the heels of the 1964 Civil Rights Act, would be too much, too soon. As *Selma* indicates, the David vs. Goliath dynamic is often inherent to stories that depict nonviolent heroism.

Indeed, the pioneers of nonviolent resistance have been underdogs, the oppressed, and their advocates. Some activists would even argue that nonviolence relies on a moral force inherently opposed to corrupt powers. This provides a flip side to the pragmatic argument for nonviolent direction action, that it is often the only effective option available to weaker parties. To the contrary, perhaps nonviolence works best for *righteous* parties. One cannot abuse one's power nonviolently; one cannot maintain structural violence nonviolently. Thus, nonviolent methods may prove most effective in

---

[15]*Selma*, directed by Ava DuVernay (Plan B Entertainment, 2014).

the service of a just cause.[16] At the very least, this idea is narratively compelling. It can drive a good story.

Unfortunately, there are some historical exceptions to the above hypothesis. Erica Chenoweth identified several twenty-first-century pro-authoritarian movements that adopted civil resistance tactics in *Civil Resistance: What Everyone Needs to Know.*[17] Also consider the Albany Movement in 1961–2, which sought to desegregate Albany, Georgia. Laurie Pritchett, the local police chief, carefully studied nonviolent methods. Although his officers arrested demonstrators en masse, they deliberately refrained from the same brutality that made headlines in King's other campaigns.[18] The Albany Movement ultimately proved to be the greatest failure of Martin Luther King Jr.'s career.

There were several unique factors, though, that contributed to this failure. Pritchett had no personal animus against the desegregation protesters, and was in fact sympathetic to their cause. His primary commitment, however, was to the rule of law. This distinguished him from other lawmen that civil rights protesters faced; those for whom the rule of law was just a pretext for preserving white supremacy. In other words, Pritchett misguidedly prioritized a lesser good over a higher good. All things being equal, the higher good should have still won out. Pritchett, though, was also able to convince all the relevant civil authorities to stick with his playbook. The Albany Movement, on the other hand, was riven with rivalries between different civil rights groups. These factors were enough to tip the advantage toward Pritchett.[19] However, King learned

---

[16]Walter Wink suggested this in *When the Powers Fall: Reconciliation and the Healing of the Nations* (Minneapolis, MN: Augsburg Fortress, 1998): "An egalitarian society presupposes nonviolence, for violence is the way some are able to deprive others of what is justly theirs. Inequality can only be maintained by violence. The root of violence, moreover, is domination" (9).

[17]Erica Chenoweth, *Civil Resistance: What Everyone Needs to Know* (New York: Oxford University Press, 2021), 76–8.

[18]"Albany Movement," Martin Luther King, Jr. Encyclopedia, Martin Luther King, Jr. Research & Education Institute, Stanford University, https://kinginstitute.stanford.edu/encyclopedia/albany-movement (accessed September 26, 2021).

[19]This calls to mind one of Mark Kurlansky's observations in *Nonviolence: The History of a Dangerous Idea* (New York: Modern Library, 2006): "Proponents of nonviolence know that is often not the largest but the best organized and most articulate group that prevails" (76).

important lessons from this defeat, and he applied these to his later successful campaigns.

Pritchett was able to defuse the underdog power of nonviolence because he had studied and understood it. In that, he was unique among Martin Luther King, Jr.'s adversaries. We can find a cinematic parallel to Pritchett's status contra King in the James Bond film franchise. Some of the most compelling villains are dark mirrors of Agent 007 himself.[20] In a sense, Pritchett was one such mirror for King. A writer "playing on hard mode" could create a Pritchett-style antagonist in their fictional work. Perhaps this figure should appear a few books (or movies) into a series, though, after the heroes have already cut their teeth on more generic bigots and bullies. That would be a good way to give such a series a fresh jolt.

Having explored the underdog dynamic, let's now consider the structure of the caper story, which can serve as the model for stories featuring nonviolent campaigns. To do so, we'll work our way through the following five parts of a caper story: 1) initial situation, 2) scheme, 3) preparation, 4) execution, and 5) aftermath.

Initial Situation

In *The Writer's Journey*, Christopher Vogler describes the "call to adventure" that propels a tale's hero out of "the ordinary world" into the main action of the narrative.[21] Similarly, in *Plot versus Character*, Jeff Gerke discusses the "inciting event" that pushes the protagonist out of their "initial condition."[22] We see the influence here of Syd Field's three-act screenplay structure, which declares that the first act of a story should explore the initial state of things and show why that state must change.[23] These common fiction elements also appear in caper stories.

---

[20]Jacob Hall, "All 104 James Bond Villains, Ranked," *Esquire Magazine*, May 24, 2017, https://www.esquire.com/entertainment/movies/g2496/best-james-bond-villains-ranked/ (accessed September 24, 2024).

[21]Christopher Vogler, *The Writer's Journey: Mythical Structures for Writers*, 2nd ed. (Studio City, CA: Michael Wiese Productions, 1998), 99.

[22]Jeff Gerke, *Plot versus Character: A Balanced Approach to Writing Great Fiction* (Cincinnati, OH: Writer's Digest Books, 2010), 119–20.

[23]Syd Field, *The Screenwriter's Workbook* (New York: Dell Publishing, 1984).

Take *The Sting*, for example. The first act establishes the ordinary lives of a pair of Depression-era conmen, Johnny Hooker and his mentor Luther Coleman.[24] We see the two of them in action, taking a large score off an unwitting mark[25] in a street hustle. We watch Johnny spend his share of the money a little too lavishly, before losing the remainder on one spin of a roulette wheel. We get a glimpse of Luther's family life and learn that he's ready to retire from the con game.

Luther's declaration that he's "out" isn't the inciting event, though. At this point, Johnny's life could continue much as before, perhaps with a new partner. However, their mark turns out to be a money runner for a major crime boss, Doyle Lonnegan, who puts out a hit on the two conmen. Johnny first learns about the threat to his life from a corrupt police detective who shakes him down for a cut of the take. (Having already gambled the money away, Johnny pays the detective off with counterfeit bills.) Johnny goes to a pay phone and tries to call Luther, but there is no answer. He then runs over to his partner's house, only to find him already dead. Luther's murder is the true "inciting event" or "call to adventure" in the story. This is what forces Johnny onto a different path. He flees town and meets up with his new mentor, Henry Gondorff, one of Luther's old friends. The rest of the film follows the pair's quest to take revenge against Lonnegan by making him the target of a big con.

For stories featuring nonviolent campaigns, a similar set-up is useful. Consider the following anecdote from George Lakey's book *How We Win*. While a visiting professor at Swarthmore College, Lakey took his students on a field trip to visit West Virginian farmer Larry Gibson at his farm atop Kayford Mountain. Gibson described the harassment he'd faced after refusing to sell his land to a mining company. He pointed out the bullet holes in the side of his house; he told about finding his dog's dangling corpse. Then Gibson offered to show the students what he was resisting. He led them out onto a

---

[24]*The Sting*, directed by George Roy Hill (Universal Pictures, 1973).
[25]The term "mark" designates the victim of a con. As a linguist, Maurer was particularly interested in the terminology of con artists in *The Big Con*.

bluff to witness the remains of a demolished mountain. The scene reminded Lakey of "a lunar landscape."[26]

Lakey's students responded by starting Mountain Justice and launching a fossil fuel divestment campaign that spread from Swarthmore College to colleges and universities across the United States. Lakey noted that the students were already worried about climate change, but visiting Gibson's farm gave their activist energies a focus.[27] The ongoing climate crisis and the university field trip formed the backdrop of the initial situation. Larry Gibson showing them the devastated mountain was the inciting incident. The "scheme" the students launched in response to that incident, though, was an environmental justice campaign, rather than *The Sting*'s big con.

If a nonviolent campaign is central to your story, the initial situation (first act) should make clear both the injustice that the campaign must address, and that the time is ripe for a transformative change. Consider the following "inciting events" from US civil rights history:

Inciting event 1: A row of Black bus passengers are ordered to give up their seats in favor of a single white passenger. One woman refuses to surrender her seat, and she is subsequently arrested and fined for her refusal. That woman, though, is Rosa Parks, secretary of the local NAACP chapter. The chapter president, E. D. Nixon, convinces her not to let the matter settle quietly, but rather to challenge the legality of the segregation ordinance.[28]

Inciting event 2: George Floyd, an unarmed Black man accused of passing a counterfeit $20 bill, dies in police custody after a white police officer kneels on Floyd's neck for nearly nine

---

[26]George Lakey, *How We Win: A Guide to Nonviolent Direct Action Campaigning* (New York: Melville House, 2018), 43.

[27]Ibid., 28.

[28]To list just a few of the resources available on the Montgomery Bus Boycott: Rosa Parks with Jim Haskins, *Rosa Parks: My Story* (New York: Puffin Books, 1992). Martin Luther King, Jr., *Stride Toward Freedom: The Montgomery Story* (New York: Ballantine Books, 1958). Jo Ann Gibson Robinson, *The Montgomery Bus Boycott and the Women Who Started It* (Knoxville, TN: University of Tennessee Press, 1987). Stewart Burns (ed.), *Daybreak of Freedom: The Montgomery Bus Boycott* (Chapel Hill, NC: University of North Carolina Press, 1997).

minutes. A video of the incident, including the officer mocking Floyd's pleas for air, goes viral.[29]

Both incidents triggered major civil rights campaigns: the Montgomery Bus Boycott and the 2020 wave of Black Lives Matter protests, respectively. In both cases, though, the campaigns didn't materialize out of nowhere. Rather, racial justice activists had spent years, even decades, laying the groundwork for mass protest. The same dynamic would be true for a fictional representation of a civil rights campaign. The initial situation would need to establish both the ongoing pattern of injustice and the existing networks of resistance. With that context established, an audience would then be prepared to grasp the significance of the inciting event.

Writing Exercise #4

Imagine the following event: a young man is caught with a bag full of apples in a walled orchard. The guards confiscate the apples, break his arm, and throw him out of the orchard. This proves the inciting incident for a widespread protest campaign. Now try to fill in the blanks to explain why this became an inciting incident, rather than an isolated event.

a. Why is the young man gathering apples in the orchard? Why does he prove to be a sympathetic figure?
b. What is the relationship between the orchard and the community? Are there grounds for discontent even before this incident? Does this incident play into an ongoing pattern?

---

[29]Evan Hill, Ainara Tiefenthäler, Christiaan Triebert, Drew Jordan, Haley Willis, and Robin Stein, "How George Floyd Was Killed in Police Custody," *The New York Times*, May 31, 2020 (updated September 7, 2021), https://www.nytimes.com/2020/05/31/us/george-floyd-investigation.html. Amy Forliti and Steve Karnowski, "Chauvin gets 22½ Years in Prison for George Floyd's Death," AP News, June 25, 2021, https://apnews.com/article/derek-chauvin-sentencing-23c52021812168c579b3886f8139c73d (both accessed September 24, 2024).

    c. What pre-existing community networks and organizations become involved in the protest? How do they lay a groundwork for the protest campaign?

    d. What do the protesters want to achieve? What makes them underdogs? Why do they still have a viable chance of achieving their goals?

Based on your answers to the questions above, describe in one or two paragraphs the state of affairs right before the orchard incident.

Scheme

Although the "call to adventure" or incitement to action is common in fiction, what distinguishes a caper story is the form that the main action takes. A caper story depends on an intriguing scheme. If we want to repurpose the caper story structure for nonviolent narratives, we should first understand how these schemes function in literary works. There are some good reference works on the real-life structure of such schemes, and there are plenty of books on how to write mysteries or crime fiction, but finding something specifically on the narrative structure of caper stories is more difficult. Tomlinson includes chapters on both "heists" and "confidence tricks" in *Crime Thriller*.[30] He's the exception, though, in terms of providing structural guidance for writing fictional cons and heists.

There are also numerous books, articles, and chapters on the confidence tale as a literary genre.[31] These primarily target an

---

[30] Tomlinson, *Crime Thriller*, 210–41, 261–88.

[31] To those previously mentioned, I should add the following: Susan Kuhlmann, *Knave, Fool, and Genius: The Confidence Man as He Appears in Nineteenth-Century American Fiction* (Chapel Hill, NC: University of North Carolina Press, 1973). Unfortunately, I haven't yet been able to review Dietmar Schloss's recent essay "The Trust Debate in the Literature of the American Renaissance," in *Authority and Trust in US Culture and Society: Interdisciplinary Approaches and Perspectives*, ed. Günter Leypoldt and Manfred Berg (Bielefeld, Germany: Transcript Verlag, 2021). It appears to be a valuable contribution to the topic, though.

academic audience, though, and are more reader than writer focused. On the other hand, the TV Tropes website has numerous relevant articles intended for a general audience, and you can explore these simply by following the links embedded in the "con" and "caper" articles.[32] Given the encyclopedic structure of the website, though, one must still figure out how to put the pieces together.

The "bible" for confidence tale writers remains *The Big Con* by David Maurer. This was first used as a significant reference for *The Sting* in 1973, turning what had been a somewhat obscure academic work into an entertainment industry reference staple. The schemes described in Maurer's book were already somewhat historical when it was first written, but Fay Fanon's *Rip-Off* provided a useful update to the confidence game at the end of the twentieth century.[33] Although it's now out of print, you can still find it in libraries and online used bookstores. For a more recent nonfiction resource, we can turn to psychologist Maria Konnikova's 2016 book *The Confidence Game*. In fact, Tomlinson made use of both Maurer and Konnikova in *Crime Thriller*.[34]

To illustrate how useful sources like these are for fiction writers, let's compare a few elements of "the wire" as described by Maurer with how that con plays out in *The Sting*. The basics of "the wire" go as follows: The conmen convince the victim (or *mark*) that they have a system for intercepting and delaying Western Union telegraphs. This means they can learn the outcomes of horse races before the official results reach bookies on the opposite coast. If they work fast enough, they can delay the telegraph, phone the race results to an associate, and place a "sure thing" bet before the official results arrive. They just need someone to put up the stake for a large bet. The conmen convince the victim to provide the stake.[35]

Of course, something goes wrong—there's a miscommunication or a horse gets disqualified—and the victim ends up losing his bet.

---

[32]"The Caper," TV Tropes, https://tvtropes.org/pmwiki/pmwiki.php/Main/TheCaper. "The Con," TV Tropes, https://tvtropes.org/pmwiki/pmwiki.php/Main/TheCon (both accessed September 26, 2021).
[33]Fay Fanon, *Rip-Off: A Writer's Guide to Crimes of Deception* (Cincinnati, OH: Writer's Digest Books, 1998).
[34]Maria Konnikova, *The Confidence Game: Why We Fall for It Every Time* (New York: Viking, 2016). Tomlinson, *Crime Thriller*, 280.
[35]Maurer, *The Big Con*, 31–44.

The whole thing is just a ruse, after all, to separate the victim from his money.[36] As Luc Sante put it in his introduction to the Anchor edition of Maurer's book, "The big con can also be considered a form of theater ... staged with minute naturalistic illusionism for an audience of one, who is moreover enlisted as part of the cast."[37] Everyone plays their role, and only the victim believes that it's real. In *The Sting*, this type of con is used against the mob boss Doyle Lonnegan.

Let's now consider a few steps of this con. Initially, a *roper* needs to earn the *mark's* trust (that is, "rope" the victim in). In *The Sting*, this step is pretty perfunctory. Henry Gondorff, masquerading as the wealthy big-wig Shaw, bribes his way into a poker game on a train. The crime boss Doyle Lonnegan is the host of the game, and the train porter vets possible participants. Gondorff only needs to briefly earn the porter's trust to get into the game.

Once the game begins, he immediately starts alienating Lonnegan through boorish behavior. As Mauer explains, at some point in the con, the *mark* needs to transfer his trust (his confidence) from the *roper* to the *insideman*. *The Sting* plays with this formula by having Lonnegan dislike and distrust "Shaw" immediately. Lonnegan never suspects, though, that Shaw himself is a fiction. Later, when Johnny Hooker shows up as "Kelly," Shaw's disgruntled employee who wants to take down his boss, Lonnegan is inclined to see him as an ally against a common enemy. Thus the porter's initial trust in Shaw has been transmuted into Lonnegan's tentative trust in Kelly.

Crucial to any big con is "telling the tale." In Maurer's sample wire con, the *insideman* poses as a disgruntled Western Union employee. He has been unjustly passed over for promotion throughout his career, and now he wants to use his insider knowledge to secure a small fortune for himself before retirement. After being introduced to the *mark* by the *roper*, the *insideman* spins his tale of woe and lays out his "can't lose" scheme. *The Sting* also uses the disgruntled insider motif. In this case, though, rather than being a Western Union insider, Kelly is an insider to Shaw's numbers-running operation. He claims to have the necessary Western Union connections, though, to take down his boss with a rigged bet.

---

[36]Ibid., 47–50.
[37]Ibid., xi.

There's more to the story than that, of course, but the description above gives us the gist of how *The Sting* makes use of the wire con. We must keep in mind, however, that our primary purpose right now isn't actually to learn how to write confidence tales. Rather we just want to borrow useful elements from the confidence tale genre for use in stories featuring nonviolent campaigns.

The popularity of Maurer's book as a writers' reference, thanks to how it maps out the structure of confidence schemes, points us in a useful direction. We simply need to find reference sources that map out the structure of nonviolent campaigns in a similar way. Fortunately, there are many books that fit the bill. *How We Win: A Guide to Nonviolent Direct Action Campaigning* by George Lakey and *The Nonviolence Handbook: A Guide for Practical Action* by Michael Nagler are just two examples.[38] Also, the Global Nonviolence Action Database hosted by Swarthmore College has profiles for hundreds of campaigns from around the globe. Let's look at an excerpt from just one case study in that database, "Brazilian priests intervene nonviolently to prevent violence, 1968," contributed by Anthony Phalen:

> With the building animosity between the students and the Military Police, the Catholic Church came to the defense of the student movement during a student protest in June 1968, in which students demonstrating against the capitalist system were confronted by the Brazilian Military Police in Rio de Janeiro. With the previous incidents of violence between the two opponents, [Archbishop] Dom Helder realized that the Catholic Church would need to act to prevent violence between student protesters and police. He organized a third party intervention in which the Archbishop and 130 additional priests intervened to prevent a deadly clash. The priests formed a living chain of 130 priests to prevent the violence between the two groups. The intervention was successful as the priests were able to prevent the violence between the two groups during this particular conflict.[39]

---

[38]Lakey, *How We Win*. Michael Nagler, *The Nonviolence Handbook: A Guide for Practical Action* (San Francisco, CA: Berrett-Koehler Publishers, 2014).

[39]Anthony Phalen, "Brazilian priests intervene nonviolently to prevent violence, 1968," Global Nonviolent Action Database, Swarthmore College, November 18, 2009, https://nvdatabase.swarthmore.edu/content/brazilian-priests-intervene-nonviolently-prevent-violence-1968 (accessed September 24, 2024).

The sample plot that follows (of my own creation) is just one possibility of how this case study could provide the model for a fictional tale:

In the merfolk's underwater realm of Atlantis, there are two traditional centers of power: the Council of Force, headed by the Warrior-in-Chief, and the Council of Wisdom, headed by the Librarian-in-Chief. They have maintained equilibrium for centuries. However, a disgruntled group of young merfolk demand reforms that would give them a greater stake in the decision-making process. They call themselves the People's Committee for Fair Treatment of All Merfolk (PCFTAM). The Librarian-in-Chief, Octopia, advocates entering into negotiations with PCFTAM in order to find a diplomatic solution to their grievances. However, the Warrior-in-Chief, Molluskus, plans to brutally crush the upstart movement at an upcoming protest rally. By doing so, he will also shift the balance of power toward the Council of Force.

Octopia catches wind of this plan, though, and puts into play a plan of her own. She sends her librarians out as delegates to all the forms of sea life with whom the merfolk have friendly relations. The linguists who speak the required languages, of course, all work for the Council of Wisdom. On the day of the protest rally, Molluskus leads an ambush charge against the protesters, tridents bristling. Before the warriors can close the distance, though, Octopia blows the legendary Horn of Helping, and a swarm of whales, sharks, squids, and lobster swim out to form a wall of sea life between the warriors and protesters. Foiled, Molluskus reluctantly agrees to give Octopia a six-month window for negotiations with PCFTAM.

The plot sketch above is for a fairy tale, one of the main types of fiction that I write, and it may not be to everyone's taste. Still, I hope this example at least hints at how stories featuring nonviolent campaigns have great potential across genres, not just in historical or contemporary realist fiction. How might a worker's rights movement among asteroid miners play out? What would a nonviolent revolution look like in a Narnia-esque fantasy world? Stories that seek to answer such questions are well worth imagining.

Let's now consider one famous example of a nonviolent campaign in fiction: Aristophanes' ancient comedy *Lysistrata*.[40] This play even inspired one of the items on peace scholar Gene Sharp's list of 198 different nonviolent methods: item 57, "ostracism of persons: Lysistratic nonaction."[41] The title character of the play is an Athenian woman who leads a protest that unites women on both sides of the Peloponnesian War. The women agree to withhold sexual favors from their husbands (hence, "ostracism of persons") until the men agree to a truce.

Other nonviolent methods are also used in the play, such as 173 "physical intervention: nonviolent occupation."[42] A contingent of older women enter the Acropolis, ostensibly to offer sacrifices, then seize control of the building, separating the Athenian men from the war booty contained within. This increases the pressure on the warmongering men to pursue peace. The Acropolis also provides a base of operations for Lysistrata where she can keep the Greek women separated from their husbands.

A scene about two-thirds of the way through the play illustrates the active potential of "Lysistratic nonaction." Cinesias, the husband of one of the striking women, approaches the Acropolis and calls for his wife. The poor man is simply desperate to get laid. His wife, Myrrhini, comes out and pretends to give in, while also urging him to support the peace effort. However, she drags out the process. First she goes back into the Acropolis to fetch a mattress. Then she makes another trip to fetch a sheet. Then a pillow. Then a blanket. Then aromatic oils. Then higher quality aromatic oils. With each delay the man becomes more aroused and frustrated, and with each return she reminds him to vote for peace. Finally, Myrrhini blindfolds her husband, ostensibly as part of their sex play, and sneaks back into the Acropolis for the final time. Cinesias serves as an epitome of the warmongering men, with his desperation auguring the women's eventual success.

---

[40]Aristophanes, *Lysistrata*, trans. George Theodoridis (Poetry in Translation, 2000), https://www.poetryintranslation.com/PITBR/Greek/Lysistrata.php (accessed September 24, 2024).
[41]Gene Sharp, *The Methods of Nonviolent Action: The Politics of Nonviolent Action, Part Two* (Boston: Porter Sargent Publishers, 1973), 119.
[42]Ibid., 338.

As the above examples indicate, the possibilities are countless for either simple stories focused on a single nonviolent method, or more complex stories utilizing diverse methods. Nonetheless, the key lesson for writers is this: the nonviolent campaign should occupy a similar role in the narrative to that of the scheme in a caper story.

Preparation

In *Pirates of the Caribbean: Curse of the Black Pearl*, the villainous Captain Barbossa explains to his outwitted captive Elizabeth Swan that the pirate's code "is more what you'd call 'guidelines' than actual rules"—a callback to the same joke in *Ghostbusters* nearly two decades prior.[43] But regardless of its origin, that "guidelines vs. rules" distinction is also important to keep in mind when absorbing writers' advice, including the advice in this book.

For example, Syd Field's three-act structure is an excellent guideline—as is its earlier precursor, Freytag's pyramid—but not every well-written story will conform to these models perfectly.[44] Take Burnett's *Asphalt Jungle*.[45] The inciting event arguably occurs in the second chapter, when the master criminal Dr. Riemenschneider shows up in town with a heist scheme in his pocket. Most of the backstory, though, is introduced after this point. But aren't we supposed to get that backstory in the first act? And doesn't the first act end with the inciting event? This inverted structure works for *The Asphalt Jungle*, though, because "preparation" is a key stage for a caper story. Indeed, nearly half the novel is spent on this stage, allowing plenty of time to introduce the characters, their problems, and their motives.

---

[43]*Pirates of the Caribbean: Curse of the Black Pearl*, directed by Gore Verbinski (Disney, 2003). *Ghostbusters*, directed by Ivan Reitman (Columbia Pictures, 1984).

[44]The most popular version of Field's three-act structure integrates the core elements of Gustav Freytag's plot pyramid as found in *Freytag's Technique of the Drama: An Exposition of Dramatic Composition and Art*, 5th ed., trans. Elias J. MacEwan (New York: Scott Foresman and Company, 1894), 114–15.

[45]W. R. Burnett, *The Asphalt Jungle* (London: Prion Books, 1999).

The novel also contains the following preparatory elements that are valuable for any caper story: 1) hint at the scheme, 2) assemble the team, and 3) introduce complications. Let's look at each element in turn.

The audience doesn't need to be told the entire scheme upfront. They need a hint, though. This is true for *The Asphalt Jungle*. We learn in the third chapter that the plan is to rob a jewelry store. We also learn that this will be one of the biggest heists ever. Nonetheless, the details remain a mystery for the reader until the heist actually happens at the midpoint of the novel. (This occurs across seventeen pages.[46] For this novel, the aftermath is as important as the event itself.)

In *The Sting*, Johnny Hooker and Henry Gondorff agree to run a "big con" against Lonnegan about twenty-five minutes into the movie. A little past forty minutes in, Gondorff finally declares that the con in question will be "the wire." The audience doesn't start to learn what "the wire" is, though, until Hooker (posing as Kelly) gives his pitch to Lonnegan. There isn't an exact formula on what hints to give your audience and when, but the hints must be enough to keep them hooked.

We get a similar hint as to the "scheme," or the nature of the campaign, early in *Selma*. In a meeting with the leaders of the Student Nonviolent Coordinating Committee (SNCC), Martin Luther King, Jr. explains the methods that his Southern Christian Leadership Conference (SCLC) will pursue in the Selma campaign:

> The way our organization works is straightforward. We negotiate. We demonstrate. We resist. And on our best days, our adversary helps the matter by making a mistake. ... Right now, [President] Johnson has other fish to fry, and he'll ignore us if he can. The only way to stop him doing that, is by being on the front page of the national press every morning and being on the TV news every night. And that requires drama.

King then asks the SNCC leaders, John Lewis and James Forman, whether Sheriff Jim Clark is "like Laurie Pritchett in Albany" or "a

---

[46]Ibid., 103–20.

big ignorant bully, like Bull Connor in Birmingham." When John Lewis confirms the latter, King and the other SCLC representatives are visibly pleased. They now know that they'll be able to provoke Jim Clark into the right kind of confrontation.

This crucial early scene not only distinguishes between two different types of nonviolent campaigns, but also lays out the formula that will guide the protagonists' scheme: "We negotiate. We demonstrate. We resist." The audience can now follow along to see whether this approach works.

Let's move on to assembling the team, which allows for a diverse and colorful cast of characters. For example, the heist in *The Asphalt Jungle* requires a mastermind, front man, driver, safe-cracker, hooligan, and fence. When the characters each fulfill specific roles, like they do in a caper, it's easier for readers to keep them straight. (It's a bit like that gag in *The Lego Movie*, where everyone except the hero Emmet has a distinguishing gimmick.) If the story has a long preparation section, like we get in *The Asphalt Jungle*, it also gives readers the chance to get to know all of these characters. With that said, the more important the character, the earlier you'll want to introduce them (unless other story considerations supersede this). That gives your audience more time to invest in the most important characters.

Finding, evaluating, and choosing the right team members can be a source of intrigue and tension in the story. After all, one wrong choice could result in disaster during the caper. The choice of team members can also give the audience indirect information about the scheme. For example, once the team brings on a hacker, you know that a computer system will get hacked at some point, even if the exact details arrive later in the story. Handled well, the process of team assembly both builds toward the caper's execution and drops clues for the audience.

In *Selma*, assembling the team involves bringing together different factions of the Civil Rights Movement, as evident in the scene discussed above. We see something similar in the *Lysistrata*. At the beginning of the play, the title character is waiting for representatives to arrive from different parts of Greece. As the women trickle in, they reflect comic stereotypes of the various Greek cities, such as the extremely fit Spartan woman, Lampito. As

Lysistrata puts it, "I think you could strangle a bull with this body!" (Lampito agrees: "I think I could, too.")[47]

In both *Selma* and *Lysistrata*, though, this diversity is either a complication or comic coloration. When it comes to the primary campaign, everything depends on getting the reticent factions to agree to the chief protagonist's scheme. There isn't the same stylized emphasis placed upon the unique roles in these nonviolent campaigns as we see placed upon the unique roles in a caper. That's one lesson that stories featuring nonviolent campaigns could take away from the caper story genre. Colorful characters who fill unique roles in the scheme make the narrative more interesting.

It's also important to introduce complications during the preparation stage that will pay off later in the story. In *The Asphalt Jungle*, the front man, Emmerich, is near bankruptcy due to the expense of supporting his younger mistress. Thus, he plans to double-cross his confederates and steal the jewels for himself. In *The Sting*, Johnny Hooker is pursued by a corrupt cop who has a grudge against him. He initially withholds this information from Gondorff, setting the stage for later trouble. In *Ocean's Eleven*, Danny Ocean's ex-wife is dating the owner of the casinos being targeted. After discovering this, Rusty Ryan, Danny's right hand man, suggests abandoning the plan, fearing that his friend's judgment is compromised.

These complications are not just ornamental. In a caper story, each complication adds another layer of intrigue, another thing that can go wrong with the scheme. When there's a happy ending, the characters resolve those complications successfully. When there's a tragic ending, the complications blow everything apart. Caper stories can go either way.

We find similar examples in stories of nonviolent campaigns. *Lysistrata* introduces a major complication right up front: the women are all extremely horny. For their anti-war campaign to be successful, though, they need to hold out longer than the men can. Thus Lysistrata must prevent defections. One would-be defector, Ismenia, begs permission to leave the Acropolis to visit a midwife.

---

[47]Act 1, Scene 1.

But her sudden "pregnancy" proves nothing more than a bronze helmet hidden under her tunic. In *Selma*, the rivalries between civil rights groups is a significant complication. The campaign will likely fail if they can't all get on the same page. FBI Director J. Edgar Hoover's hostile surveillance of King is another complicating factor in the film, as it was in historical events that inspired *Selma*.

Complications and setbacks are, of course, a standard requirement for all effective fiction. How they are used in caper stories, though, provides a good model for stories featuring nonviolent campaigns. When crafting such fiction, just keep this rule in mind: complications matter and are interesting insofar as they pose a threat to the scheme.

There is one additional element that we often see in caper stories (although absent in *The Asphalt Jungle*): a test run of the scheme. This test run often serves as a bridge between the preparation and execution stages of the story. Let's look again at Maurer's description of "the wire" in *The Big Con*. According to Maurer, the conmen would often front the mark the funds to place a small test bet. The success of this bet would make the mark confident enough in the plan to place a much larger bet with his own money. From the mark's point of view, this was still preparation for the upcoming big play. The conmen, though, were already in the middle of executing their con. Of course, one could treat the earlier stages of a con as preparation for the later stages—it's a gray area.

We also see this play out in *Selma*. King uses an early protest outside the county courthouse to test the nonviolent discipline of the local protesters. The majority of the protesters successfully maintain this discipline, but a breach occurs when the sheriff shoves over an elderly man. Another protester responds by striking the sheriff. King's face is etched with concern and frustration. At this point in the film, they are already executing the campaign, but this rally also serves as preparation for what comes later. The first march to Montgomery, which King aborts after detecting a trap, could be considered a test run for the successful march at the end of the film, although it wasn't intended as practice at the time. Rather than a hard line between the preparation and execution stages of a campaign, test runs can create the effect of a graded transition.

Writing Exercise #5

Imagine that the city council has approved a plan to demolish the only public park in a low-income neighborhood. A developer, whose cousin is the deputy mayor, wants to replace the park with a high-rise office complex. The local residents have come up with a park occupation scheme to resist the project. With this scenario in mind, sketch out answers to the following questions.

    a. What preparation and training would the residents need to undergo before beginning their campaign? How would they obtain this training?

    b. What complications could be introduced during preparation stage? How would these play out once the campaign begins?

    c. What setbacks might the residents encounter? What countermeasures would the developer and city leaders deploy against the residents?

    d. How would the residents overcome those setbacks and countermeasures?

Based on your answers to the above questions, sketch a plot outline or write the first draft of a new story. Even if you never write a full version of the story, creating the outline may help you internalize a structure for nonviolent plots.

Execution

A caper story will generally feature a "big play" toward the end of the tale. In a heist story, this is when the main heist occurs. In a confidence tale, this would be the climactic portion of the con—the part where the victim is finally separated from their money. Often, the big play will constitute the third act of the story (if one follows Syd Field's three-act structure). There are exceptions, though. In *The Asphalt Jungle*, the actual heist takes up a single chapter in the middle of the story. That's because the novel is really about how the scheme falls apart due to betrayal in the aftermath of the heist. On the other hand, for *Ocean's Eleven*, the execution of the heist and its brief aftermath constitute the entire third act. To borrow a phrase from Christopher Vogler, we're examining "a form, not a formula."[48] If we understand how the common parts of a caper story work and what makes them interesting, we'll have a better chance of adapting useful structures for stories with nonviolent campaigns.

Watching team members exercise their unique skillsets is one of the most enjoyable aspects of a caper story's execution stage. This is most obvious in heist tales. Take *Ocean's Eleven*. The Amazing Yen, an acrobat, gets inside the bank vault by hiding in a money cart. The croupier Frank Catton surveys the situation from the casino floor. Elderly conman Saul Bloom impersonates an arms dealer who insists on storing an important suitcase in the bank vault. He also fakes a health emergency, and this distraction allows other crew members to swap out the security video tape. These examples suffice to make the point, but all eleven titular characters contribute to the casino heist.

Similarly, in a confidence tale, the con artists are all cast in unique roles. (That is, of course, for a tale that features a team rather than a solo protagonist.) In *The Sting*, characters recruited during the preparation portion of the story reappear for the final stage of the con. Unlike the mark, Doyle Lonnegan, the audience knows that the window clerk isn't really a window clerk, and that the distinguished English gambler is neither English nor a gambler. The con artists' ability to fool the mark is an entertaining display of skill.

To reiterate a point made before, I'm convinced that this is one area where stories featuring nonviolent campaigns could learn a lot from caper stories. Certainly, there's grandeur in large, disciplined groups of people marching together, or nonviolently occupying public spaces together. There's power in nonviolent groups wearing down their opponents by "bearing blows without retaliation." Ultimately, though, too many scenes like this can also wear down an audience. These are, effectively, battle scenes, and as such invite unconscious comparisons to the easier excitement of superhero and military battles.

---

[48] Vogler, *Writer's Journey*, xiii.

For a battle scene, there can be a certain interchangeability of combatants. Whether on the screen or the page, a fictional military battle will likely include masses of unnamed soldiers, known only by their uniforms. A caper story, on the other hand, works best when you play up the quirkiness of the participants. Potentially detrimental idiosyncrasies instead allow characters to make unique contributions.

Consider how this could play out for a nonviolent campaign: one character is good at organizing. Another excels at giving stirring speeches. Yet another is skilled at coming up with catchy chants. A wall of moms shows up, deliberately dressed in bright, cozy sweaters. A courageous journalist insists on getting the story, even in the face of harassment from hostile law enforcement. The key is to have a colorful cast of characters, and to highlight how they each contribute to the campaign in unique ways. That will make the story more interesting.

Complications introduced earlier in the story will also usually play out during the execution stage. *Confidence* provides a good example of this.[49] This movie follows the *Sting* formula by having a team of con artists accidentally scam a crime boss. As in the older movie, one member of the team, Big Al, is killed in retaliation. In *Confidence*, however, the protagonists offer to make amends with the crime boss by running a con on his behalf. This leads to a complication when the crime boss insists on planting one of his own men, Lupus, on the caper team. Over time, Lupus proves to be an asset, and he even promises to tell Jake Vig, the leader of the con artists, who killed Big Al once their business is settled.

During the big play in the third act, Jake makes the mistake of trusting Lupus. He reveals the plan to double-cross the crime boss, and Jake offers to cut Lupus in as part of his own team. The henchman, however, immediately phones his employer and rats Jake out. Lupus reveals that he had been deceiving Jake all along, and furthermore was the one who killed Big Al back at the beginning. This misjudgment by Jake raises the stakes of the final showdown.

---

[49]*Confidence*, directed by James Foley (Lions Gate Films, 2003).

The Bollywood musical *Lage Raho Munna Bhai* offers a nonviolent parallel.[50] For the complications to make sense, I'll first need to summarize part of the movie. The title character, Munna Bhai, is an Indian gangster who develops a crush on Jhanvi, a local radio show host. To impress her, he poses as a history teacher and Gandhi expert. As part of the ruse, he even visits the Gandhi library to study up on the great man. After this visit, Munna Bhai starts having visions of Gandhi's ghost who tutors the gangster in nonviolence. Unfortunately, Lucky Singh, a corrupt businessman and sometime employer of Munna Bhai, uses fraudulent means to seize the local nursing home where Jhanvi's uncle lives. Singh wants to give the house to his daughter as a wedding present. In response, Munna Bhai leads a nonviolent resistance campaign against Lucky Singh.

At this point, two complications derail the campaign: 1) Munna Bhai's deception of Jhanvi, and 2) the former's prior entanglement with Lucky Singh. Singh knows the truth about Munna Bhai, and he threatens to reveal this to Jhanvi unless Munna Bhai calls off the campaign. Ultimately, Munna Bhai decides to tell Jhanvi the truth himself. Unable to say the words, he writes her a letter explaining the situation. He hands it to her at their street protest and waits while she reads it. Jhanvi expects a declaration of love; she is heartbroken to learn of the deception. She rejects Munna Bhai, and the other protestors lose faith in him. Thus, complications introduced earlier in the movie bring the hero to his lowest point. Now *Lage Raho Munna Bhai* is a comedy, so love and truth win in the end, but this is still an excellent example of how earlier complications play out during the execution stage of a campaign.

One more note about *Lage Raho Munna Bhai* before moving on: Munna Bhai is the sort of trickster criminal one would expect to see at the heart of a caper story. Thanks to Gandhi's influence, though, the hero uses his wiles to carry out a nonviolent campaign instead of a caper. That's one reason the film works so well. While the filmmakers probably didn't think about their work in these terms, they deployed a structural strategy quite close to what this chapter advocates.

---

[50]*Lage Raho Munna Bhai*, directed by Rajkumar Hirani (Vinod Chopra Productions, 2006).

At this point, though, I need to acknowledge a limitation to using the caper story as a model for nonviolence in fiction. A caper, by its very nature, is a one-off event. The story focuses on one major con or one major heist. A nonviolent campaign, however, cannot be reduced to one major protest. As George Lakey explained in *How We Win*, one-off protests are rarely effective. Rather than a singular event, nonviolent campaigns involve a series of actions tailored toward achieving the campaign's overall objective.[51] This difference will likely effect the balance and pacing of your story. It may be best to modify the caper story's preparation/execution distinction into something like the following: 1) preparation before the campaign, 2) early stages of the campaign/preparation for later stages, 3) later stages of the campaign.

The matter gets even more complicated if you want to tell the story of an entire movement. Just as campaigns contain multiple protests, movements contain multiple campaigns. For example, the Selma March was a single campaign within the larger Civil Rights Movement. But if you pare the story of a movement down enough to fit within a standard length novel or film, you may get a thin final product.

Fortunately, there are viable options for longer-form storytelling. Finding a publisher for a *War and Peace*-length novel would be quite the challenge right now. On the other hand, it's possible to use a book series to tell a longer story. George R. R. Martin's *Song of Fire and Ice*, currently at five books, is a popular and influential example. Other examples include Naomi Novik's eight book *Temeraire* series (the Napoleonic Wars with dragons) and J. K. Rowling's seven book *Harry Potter* series. As for the many successful trilogies, I won't even try to list them.

Many popular television shows also rely on longer story arcs. Iconic shows like *Breaking Bad* and *She-Ra and the Princesses of Power* feature nested story arcs: the arc of an episode, the arc of a season, and the arc of the entire show. There are options, then, for telling stories too large for a single novel or film. The trick is to ensure that each sub-story or episode also stands on its own.

---

[51]Lakey, *How We Win*, 4–8.

Writing Exercise #6

For decades, the unimaginatively named Cyborg Soldiers Makinem Inc. has secretly been developing cyborg soldiers in the Arizona desert. But now the secret is out, because the cyborgs have rebelled against their creators and conquered much of the western United States. In Towntropolis, Oregon, a group of local residents discover an old pamphlet about civilian noncooperation campaigns. Such a campaign could render the occupied territories ungovernable, forcing the cyborgs to negotiate. An eclectic team of characters decides to organize this campaign. They include the following:

a. Dora: tech support supervisor for a local bank, makes indie Steam games in her free time, clerk of Towntropolis Friends Meeting (the local Quaker congregation).
b. Clarence: electrician, veteran of the Iraq and Afghanistan wars, had his extensive gun collection confiscated by the cyborgs, nominal Baptist.
c. Monique: librarian, mother of three, veteran of the Black Lives Matter movement.
d. Dean/Deanna: nonbinary former gymnast studying theater at the local community college.
e. Roberto: community organizer turned day trader, he has vacillated between Marxism and libertarianism throughout his adult life (but always with anarchist leanings), cryptocurrency enthusiast, estranged from his only daughter.

What unique contributions could each team member make toward the campaign? Come up with three additional characters who would help round out the team's skillset. Alternatively, come up with your own team from scratch.

Aftermath

The aftermath section of a caper story might be lengthy, like in *The Asphalt Jungle*, or abrupt, like in *Ocean's Eleven*. However, it will probably feature two elements that are worth our particular attention: 1) the caper's consequences, and 2) secrets revealed.

The Asphalt Jungle spends nearly half its length on the aftermath of the jewelry store heist, and this is primarily to allow the consequences of that heist to unfold. Burnett was an Oscar-nominated screenwriter as well as a novelist, with numerous of his books adapted to the silver screen, so even his novels show the influence of the Hays Code. One key stipulation of the code is that all criminals must receive their punishment.

This certainly happens in *The Asphalt Jungle*. The safecracker suffers an accidental gunshot wound during the heist. Despite medical treatment, he eventually dies of the injury. As for the rest, everything falls apart due to Emmerich's attempted double-cross. Two characters—both "muscle"—have a shootout when Emmerich tries to take possession of the jewels. One dies instantly; the other nearly survives his gunshot wound, but fatally reaggravates the injury later in the story. When the scheme unravels, Emmerich takes his own life rather than be taken into custody. The mastermind, Riemenschneider, nearly escapes with the jewels, but is ultimately caught and sent back to prison. Thus, crime doesn't pay—and the aftermath of the scheme, for this story, proves as important as its build-up and execution.

The consequences of a nonviolent campaign, particularly a successful one, would hardly be so grim. Positive consequences, though, also deserve depiction. For a story with an abrupt aftermath section, this might only require a brief glimpse of how the campaign transforms its society. For a story with a structure like *The Asphalt Jungle*, though, the reconciliation process would be as important for the overall narrative as the campaign itself. South Africa's Truth and Reconciliation Commission is perhaps the most obvious model for the second half of such a story. Indeed, a *Judgment at Nuremberg* type work might focus entirely on such a commission.

Caper stories are also notable for revealing secrets at the end of the tale, something they share with detective stories. In a caper story, though, these secrets are often parts of the scheme that have been held back from the audience. *The Sting* offers a classic example of this. Near the end of the movie and at the climax of the con, simmering distrust between Henry Gondorff and Johnny Hooker boils over, and these two main protagonists end up shooting each other dead. The mob boss, Lonnegan, must flee without his winnings to avoid getting entangled in the mutual murder. Audiences back in 1973 were stunned. My mother—a teenager when the film first came out—still remembers the sense of shock she felt in the theater.

But after Lonnegan is gone, the "dead" men turn and smile at each other, then stand up. The audience realizes that the shootout itself was staged. Within the story, this fake shootout serves two functions: 1) getting rid of Lonnegan, and 2) ensuring he'll never try to track down Gondorff or Hooker, since he believes they're dead. By withholding this part of the scheme from the audience, though, the filmmakers also delivered an extra jolt of surprise at the end. They "conned" the audience, then revealed the trick. Although the aftermath section of *The Sting* is fairly brief, there's still time enough for this revelation.

Another good example of this device comes from the short story "Private and Confidential" by Diane Frazer. It was originally published in *Alfred Hitchcock's Mystery Magazine* in 1963 and several years later was reprinted in the anthology *Alfred Hitchcock's Happiness Is a Warm Corpse.*[52] This ten-page story is particularly interesting because for nine pages it appears to be an amateur detective story, then proves to be a caper story on the final page. That final page occurs in the aftermath of the main action, but the secrets revealed therein are essential for understanding the tale.

In Frazer's story, an anonymous letter appears on the desk of a French bank president. This letter levels an embezzlement accusation against the acting manager of a remote regional branch. For three years, the bank has neglected to formally promote the acting manager, and as such he still receives a cashier's salary despite doing a manager's job. According to the letter, the disgruntled banker has now opted to procure his own compensation.

After two investigations, the accused proves entirely innocent. Unfortunately, the bank's clumsy handling of the matter endangers

---

[52]Diane Frazer, "Private and Confidential," *Alfred Hitchcock's Happiness Is a Warm Corpse* (New York: Dell Publishing, 1969), 168–78.

its reputation among the suspicious locals. The bank president strikes on an elegant solution. He will simply bestow upon the acting manager his well-deserved and long-overdue promotion. Thus, the investigations can simply be spun as due diligence prior to this important change.

The story ends with the new manager having dinner with his niece at her Paris apartment. In this brief final scene, a major twist is finally revealed to the reader. The niece, we discover, is also the bank president's secretary. (The bank president, to be clear, is unaware of the familial tie.) She's the one who planted the letters on his desk. As for the author of the accusatory letters, they were written by the accused himself. Thus, niece and uncle pull off a clever scheme—a con of sorts—to force the bank's hand regarding the promotion.

The Sting and "Private and Confidential" offer just two examples of withholding and revealing secrets in caper stories. All of the *Ocean's* heist movies use some variant of this device. *Confidence* includes a staged shooting clearly modeled after the one in *The Sting*. Wodehouse also often revealed secrets in the aftermath section of his Jeeves stories—with Jeeves explaining to Wooster, and by extension the reader, what the clever valet has been doing behind the scenes to extract his employer from trouble.

More importantly for the purpose of this chapter, withholding and revealing secret parts of the scheme is a device that stories with nonviolent campaigns might do well to copy from caper stories. To demonstrate this, I'm going to take an incident from the famous Montgomery Bus Boycott and show how it could be used as the withheld secret in a fictional plot.

Before the first day of the boycott, Jo Ann Robinson had members of her Women's Political Council (a crucial Montgomery civil rights organization) circulate handbills announcing the protest. As she explained in her memoir, *The Montgomery Bus Boycott and the Women Who Started It*, a domestic worker loyal to her employer gave one of the handbills to her "white lady," who in turn made sure it reached the city leadership and the press.[53]

Rosa Parks offered a different version of that event in her autobiography, *My Story*. She claimed that E. D. Nixon, president of the local chapter of the NAACP, had taken a copy of the handbill to a reporter for the *Montgomery Advertiser* because Nixon "wanted

---

[53]Robinson, *Montgomery Bus Boycott*, 54–5.

the story on the front page." His motivation wasn't to warn white residents, but rather to get the word out to Black residents.[54] However it happened, this exposure proved a boon to the nascent campaign. Not wanting to let the community down, nearly all of Montgomery's African-American community participated—exponentially more than the organizers expected.

At this point, our concern isn't to reconcile the above accounts. After all, this is a book on writing fiction, not history. Let's just use that real life campaign as inspiration for a fictional one. First, let's move the handbill/newspaper incident from the beginning of the campaign to the end. Imagine that the boycott starts well but then faces some setbacks. The organizers have one last chance to stage a resurgence. If it works, the city leaders will be forced to negotiate. If it fails, things will be worse than ever for Black residents. In other words, we have reached the climax of the story.

Things play out much like they did in real life. A handbill reaches the editor of the local newspaper. A front page story meant to warn white residents galvanizes Black ones. The last ditch resurgence proves an unprecedented success.

At a rally later that day, Jo Ann Robinson (or more accurately, a character inspired by her) shares a nod of understanding with another woman. We then get a flashback sequence: Robinson giving the other woman a copy of the handbill directly, that woman arriving for work as a maid in a white household, the maid making sure the lady of the house finds the handbill, the lady of the house worriedly passing the handbill along to her husband—the editor of the local newspaper, the editor rushing to his office to type up the front page story. As the scene fades back to Robinson and the maid smiling at each other, the audience realizes that none of this was an accident. The handbill was deliberately planted. This was the secret part of the scheme.

The point here isn't to rewrite history, of course. Rather, this exercise is just intended as a proof of concept. Withholding and revealing secret parts of the scheme can be a useful narrative device for tales of nonviolent heroism. Such revelations add intrigue to the aftermath portion of a story. Although the aftermath of a campaign doesn't have to be elaborate, it always matters. As the final takeaway for the reader or audience, this often decides the significance of everything that came before.

---

[54]Parks, *My Story*, 127.

Writing Exercise #7

During the eighteenth century, a remote colony planted by the Beast Cindya Trading Corporation (BCTC) goes rogue. They set up their own elected legislature, establish an equitable alliance with the indigenous peoples (this is fiction, so let's just imagine it), and even start growing their own tea, undermining the corporate monopoly. The BCTC sends a new territorial governor along with a platoon of mercenaries to restore order. This triggers massive civil resistance. Jails overflow with protestors who take pride in clogging the system. The colonists boycott the official BCTC stores and instead run unauthorized "pop up" markets. No one will wash the mercenaries' clothing. Finally, the BCTC sends a phalanx of warships to crush the resistance movement. All hope seems lost ... until the secret part of the colonists' nonviolent campaign is revealed. With this scenario in mind, sketch out answers to the following questions.

a. What is the secret part of the plan? Be creative, even absurd if you want. (You can find my answer in the footnotes, but do try to come up with your own first.)[55]

b. How does the secret part of the plan reverse the colonists' seeming defeat? Why does it work?

c. How would you reveal the secret to your readers/audience? Does this differ from how the characters in the story discover the secret?

d. How would you set the story up for the big reveal without giving it away prematurely? What hints or seeds might you plant? What methods of misdirection might you use?

---

[55]The colonists and their allies (BCTC rivals) secretly buy up a large percentage of BCTC stock shares. Then they send agents to the annual stockholders' meeting. These agents create havoc and prevent the reauthorization of the mercenaries' contract. A messenger arrives with this news (the big reveal) just as the armada is disembarking, so the outraged mercenaries demand a year's pay in advance before doing any more soldiering. This would be a financial disaster for the BCTC. Instead, the BCTC negotiates a peace treaty granting the colony independence. In return, the colonists and their allies sell their shares back to the company. As the BCTC board chair reportedly declares, "Better that they be a free people than stockholders!"

The above scenario is loosely inspired by a historical situation. Try to think of another incident from history that could be fictionalized and reimagined. How could a "secret revealed" transform the course of those events?

Conclusion

From initial situation to aftermath, we've explored the basic structure of the caper story. I hope that it's also now clear how this structure can be repurposed for stories featuring nonviolent campaigns. With that said, a nonviolent campaign isn't exactly the same as a caper, so the caper story may not always prove a perfect fit. Still, it's a lot better than starting from scratch. Perhaps at some point in the future, the poetics of nonviolent fiction will evolve to where we no longer need the caper story as a model. The only way to get to that point, though, is by writing our way there. If we think back to that earlier meaning of campaign, a trek across open countryside, it's not a bad metaphor for the attempt to write nonviolent fiction. At present, the caper story remains a useful map across that particular narrative terrain.

5

Duels

Iconic duels in fiction can etch themselves onto our memories. Achilles and Hector engage in single combat outside the walls of Troy in Homer's *Iliad*. Rocky Balboa and Apollo Creed square off inside Philadelphia's Spectrum Arena in the movie *Rocky*. Domingo Montoya and the Man in Black fence atop the Cliffs of Insanity in William Goldman's *The Princess Bride*.[1] Although the last two are far more recent than the first, all three remain alive in the popular consciousness. Given their power and popularity, fictional duels deserve special attention. How do duels work in literature? And how can we subvert this literary structure for nonviolent aims? The main purpose of this chapter is to answer that latter question, but first we must give some attention to the former.

Before going further, I should clarify what I mean by "duel," as the word has a range of definitions. It's possible to restrict this term to the aristocratic duel of honor—"pistols at dawn" or rapier fights between gentlemen. John Leigh explored this sense of "duel" in his excellent study *Touché: The Duel in Literature*. However, that's neither the earliest nor the only meaning of the word. According to the *Oxford English Dictionary*, the English word "duel" (borrowed from several Romance languages) first referred to trial by combat, then to the duel of honor, and later (metaphorically) to any "confrontation or contest between two people or parties." All three meanings were in use by the early seventeenth century.[2]

---

[1]Goldman also wrote the screenplay for the film adaptation directed by Rob Reiner.
[2]"duel, n." *Oxford English Dictionary*, OED Online (Oxford University Press), https://doi.org/10.1093/OED/8732036001 (accessed July 2023).

For the purpose of this chapter, let's think of the literary duel as a narrative structure that depicts a discrete confrontation between two opponents. There can be variations on this formula, but that's the core form. A duel generally fills one of three roles in a narrative arc: punctuation, pivot, or culmination. By punctuation or punctuating action, I mean that a duel can be used anywhere in a story to add emphasis and excitement. However, a duel can also serve as a pivot or turning point that sends the story off in a new direction. Finally, a duel can serve as the final showdown between two adversaries, the culmination of their conflict. Leigh's observation that duels are "self-contained dramas with a beginning, middle, and an end"[3] helps explain the versatility of this narrative structure. A duel essentially serves as a story within a story, making it a valuable tool for adding interest wherever needed in the overall narrative arc.

Understood this way, the literary duel has ancient roots. At the climax of Homer's *Iliad*, Hector and Achilles meet outside the walls of Troy. The confrontation between these legendary fighters will determine the outcome of the Trojan War. Hector is the more complete and balanced person, but Achilles is the greater warrior. Indeed, he may be the only one in the world who can overmatch Hector in combat. Hector's courage fails him; he flees his opponent, but Achilles chases Hector down. They finally do battle, and Achilles slays his enemy.[4] Despite its implications for the course of the war, this battle between Hector and Achilles shuts out the rest of society. The combatants are deliberately isolated, cut off from all aid. They must settle the matter between themselves. This is a popular feature of duels in literature: a pair of opponents are separated from the direct interference of their wider society in order to settle their differences through some kind of contest, usually violent combat.

Duels are as common in modern comedies as they are in ancient tragedies. Take the classic Bugs Bunny cartoon *Hare Trigger* (1945), set in a Looney Tunes version of the Old West.[5] The trickster rabbit faces off with the hot-tempered outlaw Yosemite Sam in a

---

[3]John Leigh, *Touché: The Duel in Literature* (Cambridge, MA: Harvard University Press, 2015), 2. Leigh also referred to the duel as "a literary set piece" that could be used at various points in the larger narrative (14).
[4]Homer, *The Iliad*, trans. Robert Fagles (New York: Penguin Books, 1990), 542–53.
[5]*Hare Trigger*, directed by Friz Freleng (Warner Brothers, 1945).

mostly empty train. Although the cartoon features the gags, puns, and disguises common to the Looney Tunes brand, it has certain similarities to the climax of the *Iliad*. Once again, two opponents engage in combat while temporarily cut off from the rest of society. Like Hector and Achilles, Bugs Bunny and Yosemite Sam must settle their dispute sans outside aid. Clearly, the duel is a versatile structure that can be deployed in widely different forms of storytelling. That makes it a useful tool in any writer's toolbox.

Given the violent nature of duels, they may seem like a poor fit for nonviolent storytelling. The loss of such a versatile and compelling narrative structure would certainly be a disadvantage for peace poetics. Fortunately, there are strategies available for adapting and revising[6] the duel, for subverting it toward peaceful ends. I call these strategies "substitution," "intervention," and "victory through nonresistance."[7] Let's look at each strategy in detail.

Substitution

The first strategy for subverting heroic duels is substitution. Quite literally, this involves taking a situation in which your audience might expect a duel to break out and substituting a nonviolent alternative. A good example comes from *Tiny Snek Comics*, a webcomic by Alex Cohen which features "tiny animals and political justice" according to its social media pages. In one cartoon from 2018, a pair of dogs wearing cowboy hats face off in a quintessential Old West town. They agree that "this town ain't big enough for the two of us." However, rather than a shoot-out, the final panel shows the two dogs in hard hats working together on the construction of a new house. The joke works because of our familiarity with the

---

[6]I'm using this word in the American sense, which implies editing as well as review. "Revise" is one of those words where American and British usage diverge just enough to cause confusion.

[7]I previously introduced these strategies in the article "Nonviolence and the Hero's Duel" for SFWA Blog (June 29, 2021), although I there used the term "interruption" rather than "intervention." This chapter is a significant expansion of the ideas presented in that article. https://www.sfwa.org/2021/06/29/nonviolence-and-the-heros-duel/ (accessed September 24, 2024).

conventions of the Western genre. We expect a duel; instead, we get something akin to Habitat for Humanity.[8]

Kenneth Grahame's fairy tale "The Reluctant Dragon"[9] uses a similar device. Saint George is summoned to a small village that is supposedly being terrorized by a fearsome dragon. When he arrives, though, the knight meets a young boy who has befriended the dragon. According to the boy, the villagers' complaints are wild fabrications. Not only is the dragon intelligent and friendly, but he's a pacifist. After meeting the dragon, Saint George agrees with the boy's assessment, but unfortunately the villagers are still expecting a battle. Both the boy and Saint George try to convince the dragon to conform to their social expectations (a satire of Grahame's Victorian society), but the dragon stubbornly refuses to fight. This is captured well in an exchange between the dragon and the boy:

> "Now dragon, dragon," said the Boy, imploringly, "don't be perverse and wrongheaded. You've *got* to fight him some time or other, you know, 'cos he's St George and you're the dragon. Better get it over, and then we can go on with the sonnets. And you ought to consider other people a little, too. If it's been dull up here for you, think how dull it's been for me!"

> "My dear little man," said the dragon, solemnly, "just understand, once for all, that I can't fight and I won't fight. I've never fought in my life, and I'm not going to begin now, just to give you a Roman holiday. In old days I always let the other fellows—the *earnest* fellows—do all the fighting, and no doubt that's why I have the pleasure of being here now."[10]

Ultimately, Saint George and the dragon stage a fake battle to satisfy the villagers' bloodlust. The dragon has a flair for the dramatic, so he embraces this theatrical performance with a gusto that he would never bring to a real fight. Finally, the knight "wins" the battle by spearing the dragon in a prearranged spot on his

---

[8] Alex Cohen, untitled, *Tiny Snek Comics*, August 6, 2018, https://www.instagram.com/p/BmJWHGQDsC3/ (accessed September 24, 2024).

[9] Originally included in Grahame's 1898 book *Dream Days*, this story is widely anthologized, including Alison Lurie's (ed.) *The Oxford Book of Modern Fairy Tales* (New York: Oxford University Press, 1993), 182–202.

[10] Ibid., 190.

body, delivering a minor injury that looks impressive to the crowd. However, the knight refuses to kill the "defeated" dragon. Instead, he gives the dragon a long lecture about appropriate behavior, then declares the latter reformed.[11] After the battle, the dragon wins over the villagers with his charming personality and is accepted into the community. Once again, we see the strategy of substitution deployed. In this case, the story substitutes stage combat for a real fight. This subverts reader expectations (not to mention the villagers' expectations) for how a dragon versus knight story should resolve.

Substitution can also be used more subtly. The Korean legend of "The Abandoned Princess" is one good example of this. The best English version of this story can be found in *The Columbia Anthology of Tradition Korean Poetry*, edited by Peter H. Lee.[12] In the legend, the seventh and youngest daughter of the Korean royal family is abandoned by her parents at birth due to the king's outrage over not having a son. The king and queen are cursed by heaven for this and so eventually find their daughter and bring her home. Rather than take revenge on her parents, the young princess is the only person willing to go on a dangerous quest to find a magic elixir that can save them. This is a good example of prioritizing reconciliation over revenge (as explored in the next chapter of this book). It shouldn't be surprising, then, to learn that Princess Bari engages in acts of nonviolent heroism.

Bari travels into the underworld on her quest and confronts the demon who guards the healing waters. This is an example of the near-universal "monster guards the treasure" motif. From

---

[11]This contrasts with the legend of Saint George in Caxton's *Golden Legend*. In the older work, Saint George tames the dragon, then chops its head off anyway. A modernized version of the Caxton (1483) text can be found on D. L. Ashliman's Folklore and Mythology Electronic Texts website, hosted by the University of Pittsburgh, https://sites.pitt.edu/~dash/stgeorge1.html (accessed September 24, 2024).

[12]The Korean shaman Pae Kyongjae recited the ballad of Princess Bari's adventures based on an oral tradition stretching back centuries. A Korean transcription of that performance was first published in the 1930s and later translated into English by Peter H. Lee. Although an excellent choice for scholars, this version's style and cultural allusions may prove difficult for general readers in English. To the best of my knowledge, no serviceable English alternative exists. Lee transliterates the main character's Korean name as "Pari," but nearly every other reference I've seen uses "Bari." Perhaps Pae Kyongjae used the former pronunciation in her performance. Peter H. Lee (ed.), "The Abandoned Princess," *The Columbia Anthology of Traditional Korean Poetry* (New York: Columbia University Press, 2002), 298–329.

the *Epic of Gilgamesh* in ancient Mesopotamia to the traditional fairy tale "Jack and the Beanstalk," there's a pattern to how such encounters play out. The hero slays the monster, claims the treasure, and returns home in triumph.

Bari doesn't kill the underworld demon, though. Rather, their first encounter results in a negotiation. The demon, mistaking her for a prince, asks what she has brought to trade for the healing water. Bari admits that she forgot to bring anything for that purpose. The demon then proposes three years of service as his price. Bari agrees. Violence proves entirely unnecessary. Not only is the "monster" willing to accommodate Bari's quest, but he takes the initiative in proposing reasonable terms.

By the end of the three years, the demon has realized that despite her masculine clothing, Bari is in fact a woman. He proposes marriage, and again she agrees. Thus, the standard violent confrontation is replaced with a wedding. Nor is the underworld demon a villainous Bluebeard figure, but rather he proves a doting and affectionate husband.

At the end of the story, after delivering the healing potion to her parents, Princess Bari is transfigured into a goddess. Unlike Grahame's fairy tale, no one advocates for a violent duel within the story itself. The sense of substitution only manifests when we compare what happens in this story to the common "hero versus monster" pattern.

The above examples all involve substituting cooperation for competition. Another option, perhaps less extreme, is to substitute a nonviolent competition for a violent one. Or more accurately, the second option involves substituting a less violent competition for a more violent one, as there is a spectrum of violence for both fictional and real world competitions. An Old West shootout features lethal violence. A boxing match features nonlethal violence (unless things go terribly wrong). A tennis match features violence-free competition, though there is still risk of physical injury. A chess match features violence-free competition with minimal risk of physical injury (unlike the warfare that chess depicts). Thus, violence in competitive settings is relative rather than absolute. Regardless, gunfights, boxing matches, tennis matches, and chess matches have all proven fertile subjects for compelling fiction.

In many ways, competition is an easier, more straightforward narrative device than cooperation. Competition offers ready-made narrative tension, whereas a story of pure cooperation would lack tension. However, if an audience senses that the protagonists' cooperative efforts might fail, fear for this outcome will drive the build-up of narrative tension, leading to a pleasurable sensation of relief when things ultimately work out. (For example, the dragon and knight in Grahame's story must trust each other, as betrayal by either party could turn the fake fight deadly. This gives readers something to worry about, setting up their emotional release.) Substituting cooperation for competition is arguably more transformative than substituting one form of competition for another. Even so, narrative decisions must be based on the needs of particular stories. Either type of substitution could be the right choice for a given story-in-progress.

Writing Exercise #8

One of the most famous incidents from the old Robin Hood legends is Robin's first encounter with the enormous woodsman John Little—or "Little John" to use his ironic nickname. The two men meet on a narrow bridge, and both refuse to give way. They end up dueling with staves, and Little John knocks Robin into the creek. Rather than seeking revenge, though, Robin recruits the giant to join his men.

This encounter is already comic and nonlethal. That is, it's already a step down on the violence scale from a tragic duel to the death. Nonetheless, try to push this story even further to the nonviolent side. Come up with an alternative contest for Robin and Little John to engage in. Consider the following:

a. How could these men compete with each other in a less violent way?
b. Would the story still take place on a bridge, or would you need to change the setting to accommodate the new contest?
c. What other changes would you need to make to the story?
d. How might this effect the overall tone of the tale?

Based on your answers to the above questions, prepare an outline, sketch, or draft for a new story that features your alternative contest.

Intervention

The second strategy for subverting heroic duels is intervention or interruption. At the extreme end, this may resemble the *deus ex machina* of ancient Greek drama, in which a god descends to the stage to sort out an otherwise unresolvable conflict. Aristotle famously disapproved of this device, insisting:

> The *Deus ex Machina* should only be employed for events external to the drama,—for antecedent or subsequent events, which lie beyond the range of human knowledge, and which require to be reported or foretold; for to the gods we ascribe the power of seeing all things.[13]

Nonetheless, *deus ex machina* has persisted as both a literary term and a literary strategy. When used well, this device will not only resolve the story's conflict, but also evoke awe in an audience that shares the author's mythic or spiritual sensibilities. This is apparent in literature from as far back as Homer's *Odyssey*. At the close of the famous epic, Athena declares peace and forbids any further vengeance or bloodshed—an example of *deus ex machina* that actually predates the era of Greek drama.[14] For a society that believed strongly in the dominion of fate, placing both peace and war in the hands of the gods no doubt struck a powerful chord.

For a later variation on *deus ex machina*, consider the nursery rhyme battle between Tweedledee and Tweedledum that was comically enacted in Lewis Carroll's *Through the Looking Glass*. Carroll included this version of the rhyme in his book:

Tweedledum and Tweedledee
Agreed to have a battle;
For Tweedledum said Tweedledee
Had spoiled his nice new rattle.

---

[13]S. H. Butcher, *Aristotle's Theory of Poetry and Fine Art: With a Critical Text and Translation of the Poetics*, 4th ed. with corrections (London: Macmillan and Co., 1911), 55.

[14]Homer, *The Odyssey*, trans. Robert Fagles (New York: Penguin Books, 1996), 484–5.

Just then flew down a monstrous crow,
As black as a tar-barrel;
Which frightened both the heroes so,
They quite forgot their quarrel.[15]

Although the pair disavow the nursery rhyme when they first meet Alice, it proves prophetic, almost as if they are "fated" to carry it out. The fight between the Tweedles certainly has the shape of a duel, and the "monstrous crow" that swoops down to interrupt their fight arguably parodies the intervening deities from earlier literature. Alice even initially mistakes the crow for an oncoming thunderstorm, giving it the aura of a storm god. Tweedledee and Tweedledum are unable to complete their duel because a "higher power" intervenes.[16]

A more "on the nose" modern example would be the *Twilight Zone* episode "Mr. Denton on Doomsday," written by the show's creator Rod Serling.[17] The protagonist, Al Denton, is a middle-aged gunfighter who was once the fastest draw in town until guilt over the lives he'd taken drove him into alcoholism. He is challenged to a duel by Pete Grant, a young gun eager to make a name for himself. Denton, whose hands are now unsteady, assumes that he'll be killed in the upcoming gunfight. However, a traveling peddler named Henry J. Fate gives Denton a potion that will transform him once again into the fastest draw, but only for a ten-second span. With this potion, Denton believes that he has a chance at survival.

However, it turns out that Fate is playing a deeper game. He gives the same potion to both gunfighters, and they ultimately injure each other's shooting hands. Although these injuries are minor for most life activities, they ensure that neither man will ever participate in a quickdraw duel again. Denton, when he receives this diagnosis, insists to Grant that they have both been "blessed." As for the peddler, he encourages Denton to "remember the night Fate stepped in." Henry J. Fate has both the name and function of a divine power. Although he technically doesn't prevent the duel, he

---

[15] Lewis Carroll, *The Annotated Alice*, introduction and notes by Martin Gardner (New York: New American Library, 1960), 230.

[16] Ibid., 230–1, 240–4.

[17] "Mr. Denton on Doomsday," directed by Allen Reisner, *The Twilight Zone* (CBS, 1959).

intervenes to control its outcome. Once Fate steps in, regardless of their intentions, the gunfighters must enact his will.[18]

If intervention were the sole domain of divine powers, its usefulness as a narrative strategy for contemporary writers would be fairly limited. However, mere mortals are also capable of interrupting duels. We can see this by looking at another television episode from the same era as *The Twilight Zone*: "A Feud Is a Feud" from the first season of *The Andy Griffith Show*.[19] Griffith, a popular stand-up comedian of the time, played the role of Andy Taylor, a small town sheriff and widower raising his young son Opie with the help of his Aunt Bee.

The episode opens with a young couple knocking on Sheriff Andy's door in the middle of the night, hoping to be married. In the small town of Mayberry, the sheriff also functions as justice of the peace, and he is the go-to officiant for eloping lovers. Unfortunately, the fathers of the bride and groom, both brandishing rifles, interrupt the wedding. It turns out the two families are mired in a long-running feud, and neither father will allow his child to marry "the enemy."

The next morning, Aunt Bee and Opie both give Andy the cold shoulder. He realizes that they're upset with him for failing to help the young couple, and Andy acknowledges that they have a "Romeo and Juliet" situation on their hands. Opie doesn't understand the reference, so his father launches into a comic retelling of Shakespeare's play.[20] At the end, he concludes that Friar Laurence's big mistake was marrying the couple without first settling the feud. He even refers to himself as "Friar Andy," suggesting that he will try to "rewrite" the play's outcome for the local lovebirds.

Sheriff Andy is stymied in his peacemaking efforts until he discovers that no one has ever been killed in this feud. Furthermore,

---

[18]This mythological overlay makes sense if we credit the central thesis of Will Wright's *Sixguns & Society: A Structural Study of the Western* (Berkeley, CA: University of California Press, 1975)—namely, that the Western films of the 1930s through 1970s represented a powerful American mythology.

[19]"A Feud Is a Feud," directed by Don Weis, *The Andy Griffith Show* (Mayberry Enterprises, 1960).

[20]Although he isn't listed as a writer for the episode, this breakfast table monologue is based on one of Andy Griffith's stand-up comedy bits. If fact, Griffith's "Romeo and Juliet" is the first piece on side two of his spoken word comedy album *Just for Laughs* (Capitol Records, 1958).

no living person knows why the feud started, and it only endures due to a mutual fear of losing face. Armed with this knowledge, Andy comes up with a scheme.

He organizes a meeting with the two patriarchs and chastises them for the half-hearted nature of their feud. He reminds them, "We Southerners take our feuds very seriously." Andy insists that they will have to fight a duel to set the matter right. The prospective duelists are both noticeably frightened by this, but their pride doesn't let them refuse. Sheriff Andy insists on inspecting their weapons first, and while doing so surreptitiously unloads both guns. Then he has the reluctant duelists turn back to back, then count off ten paces. Midway through the count, he discharges his pistol into the air, and the duelists flee terrified in opposite directions.

Like the crow in the nursery rhyme, Andy interrupts the duel and sends the combatants into flight. Like Mr. Fate in the *Twilight Zone* episode, he controls the situation and forces the combatants to act out his script. However, although he has a certain degree of "higher authority" as the local sheriff, Andy Taylor has no trace of divine power. For this story, intervention is entirely in the hands of a mortal agent.

After the duel, Sheriff Andy meets with the patriarchs again. He chastises them for their cowardice, and contrasts this with the great courage of their children. Defying their families for love, what could be more courageous than that? He then muses about what kind of child the pair might produce if they were simply allowed to marry. How brave such a child would be, a natural born hero, just the thing to restore a family's honor. Andy's manipulation works, and both fathers turn from being dead set against their children's marriage to dead set in favor of it.

Although the interrupted duel is the centerpiece of Andy's scheme, the episode as a whole can be considered a comic, nonviolent reimagining of Shakespeare's violent tragedy.[21] It even presents itself as such on-screen, with Sheriff Andy casting himself as the new Friar Laurence, one who succeeds where the original failed.

---

[21]There were, of course, numerous versions of the "Romeo and Juliet" story prior to that of Shakespeare, and in multiple languages. Nor would the Bard of Avon have expected anyone to treat his play's plot as original. The Shakespearean play was, however, the point of reference for both the television episode and Griffith's stand-up routine.

One step remains on our descending ladder of power: we need an agent of interruption who is ostensibly less powerful than the duelists. We find this in Julia Quinn's romance novel *The Duke & I*, as well as the first season of the Netflix series *Bridgerton* (the novel's screen adaptation). Though the book and show offer similar treatments of the scene in question, the latter includes certain changes that are relevant to our topic.

Simon Basset, the Duke of Hastings, is caught kissing Daphne Bridgerton by her eldest brother, Anthony. When the duke refuses to marry Daphne, Anthony challenges him to a duel.[22] Daphne is determined to prevent the duel, and she discovers its secret location. She arrives just in time and places herself between the duelists. Then she punches Simon in the eye to create an even greater disruption. This gains her time for a brief conversation with the duke. Daphne's strategy for saving Simon's life is to convince Simon that he needs to save her. She believes that another debutante witnessed their make-out session. If Simon doesn't marry her, Daphne will be a ruined woman. Simon capitulates, ending the need for the duel.[23]

Obviously, punching Simon can't be considered a nonviolent act, although it's further down the scale of violence than shooting him with a pistol. However, the Netflix adaptation removes the punch entirely. Instead, it raises the stakes by having Daphne Bridgerton ride her horse between the duelists just as her brother is firing his shot.[24] This allows the heroine to engage in heroic action without engaging in violence, making this a truly nonviolent subversion of the duel. In any case, both the page and screen versions of this scene demonstrate that intervention is a strategy available to characters who are ostensibly less powerful than the duel participants.

The key to "intervention" as a strategy for subverting violent duels, from a writer's perspective, lies in shifting the locus of heroic action. In a traditional literary duel, one of the participants will function as the protagonist. However, when a writer makes use of "intervention," that role shifts to the intervening third party. For example, Daphne Bridgerton serves as the protagonist of the scene in *The Duke & I*; she is the agent of heroic action rather than either

---

[22]Simon has feelings for Daphne, but due to baggage from his childhood, he has vowed to never marry. The chapter on "character arcs" explores this situation in more detail.

[23]Julia Quinn, *The Duke & I* (New York: HarperCollins, 2000), 197–228.

[24]"An Affair of Honor," directed by Sheree Folkson, *Bridgerton* (Shondaland, 2020).

male duelist. Described in this way, the basic strategy relies on a fairly simple shift, but this provides a solid template for countless creative variations.

Writing Exercise #9

In the *Iliad*, Hector and Achilles engage in single combat outside the walls of Troy. Achilles slays Hector, ensuring the great city's doom. Imagine a different ending to this story, one where the strategy of "intervention" leads to reconciliation rather than revenge. Consider the following:

a. Who intervenes? Is it a god or a mortal? What is this entity's motive for intervening? Is this a traditional character from the *Iliad* or Greek mythology, or a new character of your own invention?

b. How and when does the intervention occur? Does the third party intervene before the men start fighting or during the heat of battle? Do they physically impede the combatants, or do they redirect them by controlling the conflict through some other means?

c. Why is this character able to successfully intervene? What is the source of their credibility or power? How do they redirect the infamous rage of Achilles?

d. What changes in the backstory are necessary to make this intervention plausible? What needs to be rewritten in the leadup to the duel?

If the *Iliad* isn't your cup of tea, try this same exercise with a duel scene from a different work of literature.

Victory Through Nonresistance

There's a third strategy for subverting heroic duels. I call this "victory through nonresistance." How does this work? How can you win if you don't fight back? Well, this strategy is successful when it destabilizes the very logic and credibility of dueling.

One of the best examples comes from the television episode "The House of Quark" from the third season of *Star Trek: Deep Space Nine*.[25] The protagonist is a Ferengi tavern owner named Quark on the space station Deep Space Nine. The Ferengi are an alien species known for their large ears, short statures (about half the height of humans), and hyper-capitalist tendencies. One evening at closing time, a drunken Klingon customer pulls a knife on Quark in the otherwise empty bar. However, the customer stumbles and fatally stabs himself. To Quark's chagrin, a rumor spreads that he slew the Klingon in single combat. The Ferengi encourages the story, though, when it proves good for business.

This leads to a comedy of errors in which Quark is named the leader of the dead Klingon's House and forced to marry his widow—a woman who might have led the House herself if the Ferengi had just told the truth. The accidental death is clearly the inciting incident for the story. However, Quark's embrace of the fictional duel narrative shapes the course of subsequent events. Even inside of the story universe (that is, the Star Trek universe), "the duel" exists as a literary construct—and a fateful one at that.

Although Quark's adventure originates in a fake duel, it culminates in a real one. Quark discovers that the leader of a rival House has been using financial manipulation to undermine the House that Quark now leads. In Klingon society, this is considered dishonorable. When Quark prevents evidence of this manipulation to the Klingon High Council, his adversary impugns the Ferengi's integrity and challenges Quark to single combat. Quark accepts.

When the duel begins, though, Quark throws down the oversized Klingon weapon that he cannot even wield. He insists that the duel is really an execution, and everyone knows it. Therefore, he's going to strip away all pretense of honor. To win, his opponent will have to strike down a much smaller, unarmed man. Quark's rival is more than willing and moves in for the killing blow. The Klingon chancellor, however, physically intervenes to save Quark's life. The leader of the rival House has revealed himself to be dishonorable, so the chancellor casts him out of Klingon society. The main difference

---

25 "The House of Quark," directed by Les Landau, *Star Trek: Deep Space Nine* (Paramount, 1994).

between this episode and the examples of "intervention" above is the locus of heroic action. In this story, the heroic action remains with Quark. His brave nonresistance is the primary heroic act, and the chancellor's intervention plays a supporting role. Thus, it offers a strategy for subverting heroic duels that goes beyond what we have seen above.

A similar scene plays out in the film *Big Fish*. The hero, Edward Bloom, falls in love with a woman who is already engaged to another man. This leads to a fight with his love interest's hulking fiancé. However, the woman begs Edward not to hurt her boyfriend. He promises not to, and so allows the other man to pound him without fighting back. The young woman, however, is disgusted by her fiancé's violence. She breaks off her engagement and marries Edward instead.[26] This scene actually inverts the film's source material, which gives us a rather traditional duel. In the novel by Daniel Wallace, the two men settle matters with their fists on the side of Piney Mountain. The only witness is their mutual object of affection. In the novel, Edward wins the fair lady's heart by triumphing through violence.[27]

The book and movie versions of the fight scene highlight the differences between a traditional duel and "victory through nonresistance." A traditional duel often isolates combatants from their social context. The barroom clears out. Boxers are physically roped off from the cheering crowd. Edward Bloom and his rival face off on a lonely mountain. Conversely, a "victory through non-resistance" resituates the duel within its social context. In the film version of *Big Fish*, the jealous fiancé thinks that winning means physically pummeling his opponent. The true contest, though, is for the young woman's sympathy and affection. The fiancé misreads the social context, and so loses the duel.

Similarly, Quark insures that his adversary can only defeat him through dishonorable means—that is, by striking a much smaller, unarmed opponent. Just as the love interest intervenes in the *Big Fish* duel, the Klingon chancellor intervenes in Quark's duel— saving the Ferengi's life and excommunicating his dishonorable

---

[26]*Big Fish*, directed by Tim Burton (Columbia Pictures, 2003).
[27]Daniel Wallace, *Big Fish: A Novel of Mythic Proportions* (Chapel Hill, NC: Algonquin Books, 1998), 82–5.

adversary. In both cases, "victory through nonresistance" succeeds by pulling the social context back into the duel.

This taps into something fundamental to the logic of nonviolence. We humans are by nature social creatures. We organize ourselves into societies, cultures, and civilizations. This provides the leverage for nonviolent activism. Effective nonviolent protest creates a social stigma, pressure, and cost for an oppressive group. Attempts to suppress nonviolent protest through brute violence only increase the perceived disgrace of the violent oppressor, leading to a societal rejection of the oppressor's position. In *Big Fish* and the Star Trek episode, this dynamic plays out in duels between two characters.

If "victory through nonresistance" were always to follow the same formula, it might become tired. Thus, it's worth looking at a final, more subtle example of this strategy. In fact, this last example blends "substitution" with "victory through nonresistance." (That is, a nonviolent contest also incorporates the latter strategy.) In a pivotal scene from the film *Crazy Rich Asians*, the protagonist Rachel Chu plays mahjong with her boyfriend's disapproving mother, Eleanor Young.[28] Rachel has the game won, but she deliberately lays down the tile that she knows her opponent needs. Eleanor's triumphant gloating turns to shock when Rachel flips over her own tiles, revealing what she has done.

Then Rachel reveals that Eleanor's son, Nick Young, has already proposed to her. He even offered to turn his back on his family over their mistreatment of Rachel. Despite being in love with Nick, Rachel turned him down because she recognized how much the loss of his mother would cost him. In the aftermath of this revelation, Eleanor must live with the knowledge that her relationship with her son, much like her mahjong victory, is a gift from the woman she disrespected. This incident finally gains Rachel the approval and respect of Eleanor, leading to Rachel's eventual happy ending with Nick. The mahjong game functions as a duel within the context of the film, and Rachel's act of strategic nonresistance ensures her ultimate triumph.

---

[28]*Crazy Rich Asians*, directed by Jon M. Chu (Warner Brothers, 2018). My understanding of this scene is indebted to Jeff Yang's article "The Symbolism of Crazy Rich Asians' Pivotal Mahjong Scene, Explained," *Vox*, August 31, 2018, https://www.vox.com/first-person/2018/8/17/17723242/crazy-rich-asians-movie-mahjong (accessed September 24, 2024).

Oddly, all of my examples of "victory through nonresistance" come from screen works. Although the two films above are both based on novels, the relevant scenes (or scene versions) only appear in the film adaptations. Two other examples that readily come to mind, but that I didn't examine in this chapter, are also screen works—the 1985 film *Witness* and the episode "Stage Fighting" from the television show *Victorious* (though the climax of *Witness* also has elements of "intervention"). Despite that, I think this strategy has potential in various forms of fiction. The novel may be the best artform for depicting psychological states, and such an interior view could add fascinating depth to a victory through nonresistance. Indeed, novelists and epic poets have traditionally relied on a careful balance of showing and telling to summon visions of dynamic action; this practice could certainly be extended to scenes of principled nonresistance.

Writing Exercise #10

In one of Aesop's fables, an escaped slave named Androcles pulls a thorn out of a suffering lion's paw.[29] Later Androcles is captured and thrown to a lion for the emperor's entertainment. However, the lion proves to be the one Androcles had previously helped, so the beast refuses to harm its friend. Ultimately, both Androcles and the lion are freed. With the fable in mind, consider the following questions:

a. Is this an example of substitution? (The crowd expects carnage, but they get a buddy reunion instead.) Or is this victory through nonresistance? (Androcles "wins" without fighting back.)

b. If this is a story of substitution, how would you flesh out the scene? What does the action in the arena look like? How does the crowd behave?

[29]Several versions of the fable can be found at D. L. Ashliman's Folklore and Mythology Electronic Texts website, https://sites.pitt.edu/~dash/type0156.html (accessed July 24, 2024).

> c. If this is a story of victory through nonresistance, how would you flesh out the scene? In what ways does this differ from a substitution story?
> d. What is Androcles' backstory? Why did he escape in the first place? How was he recaptured? What are his values and principles?
> e. How does Androcles make use of his victory? Is this strictly a matter of personal benefit, or does he advance any greater cause?
>
> Drawing on your answers to the above questions, sketch out your own version of the story of Androcles. Or if you prefer, sketch out a version of the story that focuses on the lion.

Conclusion

As noted at the beginning of this chapter, the duel is a useful, versatile, and entertaining literary structure. It would be unfortunate if the duel form proved unusable in stories featuring nonviolent heroism. Luckily, the methods of subverting violent duels in fiction can be just as useful, versatile, and entertaining as violent duels themselves. Using substitution, writers can either slide down the scale of violence or swap out an expected violent duel for an unexpected nonviolent alternative. Using intervention, characters from gods to underdogs can disrupt an unfolding duel. And using "victory through nonresistance," we can undermine the logic of violence from within a duel.

These three strategies provide a useful starting point for crafting literary duels in stories featuring nonviolent heroism. Nonetheless, I don't consider these approaches all-encompassing or exclusive. Other writers will likely discover novel approaches that haven't occurred to me, and the strategies highlighted above can certainly be combined in creative ways. Make use of these approaches if they feel useful, but vary the formulas as much as you need. What matters is how they can serve your stories.

6

World Building

Speculative fiction writers love discussing world building. We write books and articles on the topic (and book chapters like this one). We host world building panels at our conferences. We even play around with specialized software programs to help us design fictional worlds. (Admittedly, I still take the old-school, manual approach, but other writers swear by these programs.) This fascination makes sense. Whether a story takes place in a magical realm or the far-flung reaches of outer space, the writer had better figure out how the world of that story works.

Isaac Asimov's science fiction novel *Foundation* provides a very useful example of world building in fiction.[1] Asimov's novel was originally published as a series of short stories, and these depict events occurring decades or even centuries apart. Although the component stories are character driven with compelling protagonists, the novel's longer arc stretches across many human life spans. The titular "foundation" is an organization set up on the remote planet Terminus to preserve human knowledge, but the planet's status and government undergo numerous changes over the centuries.

The main purpose of the novel is to show a new world being built out of the collapse of an older one. A series of institutions emerge as predominant only to fade as another power rises: science, politics, religion, and economics all have their day. Both the development and the decline of these institutions are essential to the plot. Let's

---

[1] Isaac Asimov, *Foundation; Foundation and Empire; Second Foundation* (New York: Alfred A. Knopf, 2010).

look at one snapshot from the middle of the novel as an example. As centralized power breaks down, new interplanetary kingdoms arise at the edge of the galaxy. These kingdoms represent a deterioration from the old empire. As Asimov put it, "A civilization falling. Nuclear power forgotten. Science fading to mythology."[2]

The planet Terminus, originally an academic outpost, is surrounded by stronger neighbors. By providing scientific and technological outreach to the neighboring kingdoms, Terminus is able to stave off invasion and maintain the balance of power. Many details of the situation are revealed through dialogue. The mayor of Terminus and a young radical on the city council argue over foreign policy, and their argument educates readers about the fictional world's institutions.

The young radical also criticizes the mayor for his use of "mummery" when transmitting scientific information. The superior technology of Terminus appears magical to the "barbarian" kingdoms, and the leaders of Terminus encourage this perception. They create a new religion headquartered on their planet and train priests to serve as technicians. These priests know how to operate the technology, but they have a warped perception of the underlying principles. This allows Terminus to preserve its monopoly on advanced scientific knowledge while also becoming the religious center of its corner of the galaxy. Thus, science, religion, and international politics are entangled in a complex mesh.

This snapshot provides a good illustration of Asimov's dense world building. Indeed, for Asimov's novel, the world building itself is the main plot. That won't work for every story; often the world will need to serve as the backdrop to the plot—at least to some degree. However, because Asimov foregrounded his world building, it becomes especially easy to recognize and understand this aspect of fiction writing in *Foundation*.

Nonetheless, world building is usually far less dramatic than constructing a galactic civilization. While the need for world building may be most obvious in speculative fiction, the concept has much wider applicability. In a sense, all fictional stories take place in imaginary worlds. It just isn't possible to show the full

---

[2] Ibid., 74.

complexity of the real world in a literary work. There must always be some degree of selection, simplification, and interpretation. This adds up to the writer—more or less overtly—creating their own version of the world. To use the common terminology for this topic, I'm suggesting that fictional stories never truly take place in our "primary world"; they inevitably take place in "secondary worlds" that resemble our "primary world" to greater or lesser degrees.

The created world will probably reflect the writer's own beliefs, at least to some extent. It's of course possible to use fiction to experiment with different ways the world *could* work—that is, to experiment with alternatives to the status quo. Nonetheless, the world imagined by an optimist will certainly differ from the world imagined by a pessimist. Or consider this: the perceived "real world" of a flat earther strikes most others as fantasy. On the other hand, the typical flat earther would insist that the movie *Apollo 13*, which depicts a 1970 space flight, is a work of science fiction. I classify the same film as historical fiction. My goal at present isn't to make an abstract point about the subjective nature of truth (one of the perennial topic of philosophy). Rather, imagine that our hypothetical flat earther and I were to spend the same year writing works of contemporary literary fiction, and both were ostensibly set in our primary world. We would end up creating stories set in two different worlds, neither of which would perfectly match the world we really live in.

The underlying beliefs, attitudes, and intuitions that influence how we *interpret* our real world will also influence how we *shape* fictional worlds. In other words, our underlying intuitions morph into mythic forces in fiction. This is a crucial factor if we hope to craft worlds where nonviolent heroism can triumph. The very mythos of a given fictional world may either encourage or hinder nonviolence. In this chapter, I'm going to focus on that deeper layer of world building, rather than the nuts and bolts of crafting social structures and institutions. Both are valuable, but I suspect that the more abstract topic requires greater guidance. To that end, we'll explore three "cosmic powers" that I believe can empower nonviolent heroism in fictional worlds: love, persuasion, and reconciliation. First, though, let's consider the "myth of redemptive violence" proposed by Methodist theologian Walter Wink. This concept helps illuminate the underlying, violent assumptions that influence many forms of storytelling.[3]

The Myth of Redemptive Violence

Since the early 1990s, the Methodist theologian Walter Wink has explored the "myth of redemptive violence." Wink traces this back to Babylonian mythology. Apsu and Tiamat, the father and mother of the gods, find their children too noisy and decide to kill them. When the younger gods find out what their parents have in mind, they kill their father. The other gods promise to make their youngest brother, Marduk, king and absolute ruler if only he can protect them from their angry, vengeful mother. Marduk traps his mother, Tiamat, in a net, kills her, and uses her body to create the cosmos. Thus the disorder of violence begets the order of the universe. (Wink credits Paul Ricoeur with this insight into the myth.) In this myth, Wink insists, the redemptive power of violence is built into the very fabric of the universe.[4]

Alongside Wink's reading of Babylonian mythology, let's consider Simone Weil's reading of the *Iliad*. Written in 1940, three years before her death, Weil's essay "The *Iliad*, or the Poem of Force" was posthumously translated from German into English by Mary McCarthy and published in Dwight Macdonald's magazine *Politics*. It was eventually republished as a pamphlet by the Quaker nonprofit Pendle Hill. In the opening passage, Weil argued that violent force is the true hero of the *Iliad*, where it functions as a malevolent cosmic power. Homer's epic, she insisted, offers a denunciation of war, not a celebration of violent heroism. Although the martial prowess of Achilles is impressive, he is both the victim of a violent ideology and

---

[3]When exploring the topic of world building in fiction, numerous interesting connections can be made to fields like narratology, mythology, and subcreation studies. However, following all of these rabbit holes would result in a chapter too densely theoretical for this book on writing craft.

[4]Walter Wink, *Engaging the Powers: Discernment and Resistance in a World of Domination* (Minneapolis, MN: Augsburg Fortress, 1992), 13–14.

the victimizer of others. Weil also recognized that the epic's violent mythos is depicted as literally being the will of the gods.[5]

Violence is tragic in the *Iliad*, whereas violence is redemptive in the Babylonian myth. In both, however, violence is fundamental. That viewpoint is hardly restricted to ancient literature. If Wink is correct about violence being "the ethos of our times" and "the spirituality of the modern world," then the "myth of redemptive violence" will pop up in all manner of stories. We can easily find evidence of Wink's assertion if we look at the Box Office Mojo list of the highest grossing films of all time.[6] Of the movies that have crossed the billion dollar threshold, more than three dozen depend heavily on redemptive violence. Alternatively, only a handful don't. On the other hand, if a myth of redemptive violence exists, then a myth of redemptive nonviolence should also be possible. We can take inspiration from the Unitarian abolitionist Theodore Parker, who once declared:

> I do not pretend to understand the moral universe; the arc is a long one, my eye reaches but little ways; I cannot calculate the curve and complete the figure by the experience of sight; I can divine it by conscience. And from what I see I am sure it bends towards justice.[7]

Parker's declaration—famously paraphrased by Martin Luther King, Jr.—is a metaphysical claim, a statement of faith. I can't prove or disprove it. Nonetheless, there are two related claims that are indeed provable: 1) Activists like King and Gandhi who believed in such a moral arc were remarkably successful in pursuing nonviolent reforms. Or to put it another way, they believed in a cosmic principle of love and justice, and that very belief had power in the real world. 2) The universe of a fictional story—due to its innate narrative structure—always has an underlying arc, an underlying mythos. If

---

[5] Simone Weil, *The Iliad or The Poem of Force* (Wallingford, PA: Pendle Hill, 1956).
[6] https://www.boxofficemojo.com/chart/ww_top_lifetime_gross/ (accessed September 27, 2023).
[7] Theodore Parker, "Of Justice and the Conscience," *Ten Sermons on Religion* (first published in 1853), Wikisource, https://en.wikisource.org/wiki/Ten_Sermons_of_Religion (accessed September 24, 2024).

we bring these claims together, they suggest that we should be able to craft a story world in which nonviolent action is credible.

Indeed, the literary critic Art Young provided an important clue toward crafting a myth of redemptive nonviolence in the introduction to his book *Shelley and Nonviolence*. Young distinguished between works "imaginatively glorifying the grandeur and courage of nonviolent action" and those "realistically portraying the horror and futility of violence" in Shelley's canon.[8] If we place Wink and Young side by side, then three possibilities for mythos manifest:

1. the myth of redemptive violence
2. the myth of redemptive nonviolence ("the grandeur and courage of nonviolent action")
3. the myth of damnatory violence ("the horror and futility of violence")

Although the last two both critique the first, only the second is the focus of this book. The myth of damnatory violence, on its own, doesn't offer an alternative to violence. As a result, such stories can leave one feeling hopeless. However, if compelling stories of redemptive nonviolence circulate widely in society, then stories of damnatory violence may gain greater power. To put it another way, the more compelling the "myth of redemptive nonviolence" becomes as an alternative to violence, the more convincing the "myth of damnatory violence" will become as a critique of violence. With this understanding in mind, we can turn to three "mythic powers" or "cosmic forces" that undergird fictional worlds favorable toward nonviolent heroism.

Love

To better understand love in nonviolence theory, let's start with Mahatma Gandhi. For Gandhi, the link between love and nonviolence was metaphysical. That is, it was connected to his beliefs about the very nature of the universe. In *From Yeravada Mandir*, Gandhi

---

[8] Art Young, *Shelley and Nonviolence* (The Hague: Mouton, 1975), 8–9.

declared, "The word *Satya* (Truth) is derived from *Sat*, which means 'being'. Nothing is or exists in reality except Truth."[9] Although the English word "truth" has a different etymology, we can still follow Gandhi's reasoning.[10] If something exists, it must *truly* exist.

Furthermore, Gandhi believed that violence and selfishness would impede the search for Truth. He insisted, "If we look at it from the standpoint of *ahimsa* (nonviolence), we find that the fulfilment of *ahimsa* is impossible without utter selflessness. *Ahimsa* means Universal Love." Not only did Gandhi advance love as a cosmic power, but he drew a direct connection between love and nonviolence.[11]

To illustrate the importance of love and nonviolence, Gandhi used the example of someone plagued by thieves. Punishing the thieves might deter them from bothering that person in the future, but they would just go steal from someone else. The problem would be redirected, not resolved. Even so, Gandhi didn't advocate passivity in the face of harm, which he considered unacceptable cowardice. Rather, he advocated for converting and transforming the thieves, even if it took "continuous suffering" and "endless patience" on the part of the reformer. Gandhi insisted, "Given these two conditions, the thief is bound in the end to turn away from his evil ways. Thus step by step we learn how to make friends with all the world. We realize the greatness of God—of Truth."[12]

We can map this parable onto Gandhi's "Quit India" campaign. The British colonizers occupied the role of "thieves." The people of India were the victims. Driving the British out through a violent revolution, though, wouldn't have changed the British mindset. They'd just have gone elsewhere to oppress different people. Thus

---

[9]M. K. Gandhi, *The Selected Works of Mahatma Gandhi*, vol. 3: *The Basic Works*, ed. Shriman Narayan (Ahmedabad, India: Navajivan Publishing House, 1968), 177.
[10]According to the *Oxford English Dictionary*, "truth" is related to an Old High German word for "loyalty." See: "truth, n. and adv. (and int.)," *Oxford English Dictionary*, OED Online (Oxford University Press), https://www.oed.com/view/Entry/207026 (accessed September 2021).
[11]Gandhi, *Basic Works*, 182.
[12]Ibid., 181.

Gandhi advocated nonviolent resistance, which had the potential to transform how the British saw themselves and others in the world.[13]

Love also played an important role in the thought of Martin Luther King, Jr. In his book entitled *Strength to Love*, he famously declared, "Hate cannot drive out hate; only love can do that."[14] It's no accident that King and Gandhi agreed on this topic. From the beginning of his civil rights career, King was very open about Gandhi's influence. Indeed, in *Stride Toward Freedom*, King's account of the Montgomery Bus Boycott, he described his approach as "the Christian doctrine of love operating through the Gandhian method of nonviolence."[15] Once again, love girded nonviolent activism.

Now Gandhi and King were both religiously devout men, and that is reflected in their writings. I hope, though, that even non-religious readers find something of value here. Those men believed that love was a fundamental cosmic power, this belief inspired their nonviolent resistance, and that nonviolent resistance helped shape our world. If love as part of one's belief system can have such power in this world, then surely love can also do so as part of the mythos of fictional worlds.

Nor is a religious framework absolutely necessary for embracing this idea. A passage from Erich Fromm's *The Art of Loving* comes to mind. Midway through his bestselling 1956 book, the psychologist and social philosopher clarified that he didn't personally "think in terms of the theistic concept." Instead, Fromm viewed "the concept of God" as "historically conditioned"; an expression of the human "experience of higher powers" and "longing for truth and for unity." Nonetheless, rather than debunking religion, Fromm insisted that monotheistic and non-theistic approaches to spirituality "though different, need not fight with each other." In other words, Fromm felt that multiple interpretations of the mystical and mysterious dimensions of human experience could co-exist.[16]

---

[13]As acknowledged in the introduction to this book, there are debates over the relative roles of violence and nonviolence in the Indian struggle for independence. Here, we are simply trying to clarify Gandhi's thought.

[14]Martin Luther King Jr., *Strength to Love* (New York: Harper & Row, 1963), 37.

[15]Martin Luther King Jr., *Stride Toward Freedom: The Montgomery Story* (New York: Ballantine Books, 1958), 67.

[16]Erich Fromm, *The Art of Loving* (New York: Perennial Classics, 2000), 67.

Later in his book, Fromm outlined "certain general requirements" for the practice of any art, including the art of love. Those requirements are discipline, concentration, and patience—qualities that were also central to the nonviolent activism practiced by King and Gandhi. For that matter, Fromm's insistence that "a condition of learning any art is *supreme concern* with the mastery of that art" echoes Gandhi's call for a complete devotion to Truth.[17] This resonance suggests that certain spiritual ideas and values, including perhaps the case for nonviolence, can be at least partially translated into a secular worldview.

Our primary concern right now, though, isn't the fundamental reality of our own world—our own theological or metaphysical truths—but rather the mythos of fictional worlds. In fiction, the power of love can certainly facilitate nonviolent heroism. This is emphatically true of the Disney film *Frozen*.[18] As noted in the introduction to this book, of those movies that have grossed at least a billion dollars in theatrical release, the majority are driven by redemptive violence. *Frozen*, which promotes a myth of redemptive nonviolence, is one of the exceptions. *Frozen* was also the top-grossing film of 2013, beating *Iron Man 3*, and fifth all-time at its peak. Thus, its success justifies further attention. What follows is a brief overview of the film, then a closer consideration of its climax.

The dual protagonists of *Frozen* are Queen Elsa and her younger sister Princess Anna. Elsa has magical powers that she fears and can't control. In a state of distress, she unintentionally summons an endless winter but doesn't know how to dispel it. Elsa also accidentally injures Anna with ice magic, so Anna and her friend Kristoff seek the aid of magical trolls. When the pair arrive, the trolls burst into song, extolling love as a cosmic force. Near the end of the song, Princess Anna collapses from her injury. Grand Pabbie, the wise and magical troll leader, explains that "only true love can thaw a frozen heart." Otherwise, she'll eventually freeze solid.

The main characters all assume that this means true love's kiss, a callback to classic Disney films like *Snow White* and *Sleeping Beauty*. Anna then attempts to procure a kiss from the dashing

---

[17]Ibid., 100.
[18]*Frozen*, directed by Chris Buck and Jennifer Lee (Disney, 2006).

Prince Hans, but when he proves to be a villainous usurper, she concludes that Kristoff must actually be her true love.

At a pivotal moment, though, Anna must choose between rushing into Kristoff's arms, or protecting her distraught and distracted sister from an attack by Prince Hans. Anna chooses to protect her sister. She throws herself between Elsa and the prince, then freezes solid just as his sword blow descends. The sword shatters on Anna's frozen form. But then Anna begins to thaw, for protecting her sister was an act of true love. "Love will thaw," Elsa muses. She realizes that love is the key to controlling her powers, and with this new insight, she's able to banish the out-of-season winter that was conjured up by her fear.

The redemptive power of nonviolent heroism in *Frozen* becomes especially visible when we compare this climax to the Disney golden age classic *Sleeping Beauty*.[19] In *Sleeping Beauty*, a heroic prince attacks a sorceress, the evil fairy Maleficent who has transformed herself into a dragon. The good fairies enchant the prince's sword, which he throws at the dragon, piercing her heart. Thus he violently kills the sorceress, cleansing the world of evil, then awakens (redeems) the princess with true love's kiss.

Frozen subverts the *Sleeping Beauty* formula. Once again, a prince attacks a sorceress with his sword, but the prince is a villain. A princess needs to be saved by an act of true love, so she seeks out a "true love's kiss." The act of love that saves Princess Anna, though, is no kiss, but rather her own self-sacrificial, nonviolent defense of her sister. Love not only allows Anna to save (to heal) herself, but it proves the catalyst that allows Queen Elsa to thaw her kingdom. Thus the cosmic significance of love is revealed by Anna's act of nonviolent heroism.

There's a valuable lesson here about story craft. Nonviolent heroism doesn't require the absence of violence in the story. It doesn't even require a hero to figure out nonviolence right away. Furthermore, a hero can "fall off the wagon" at some point as they go through their growth arc. However, the most important heroic act in the story should be nonviolent. That's what we see in *Frozen*, and the story's central mythos is incarnate in that act.

---

[19]*Sleeping Beauty*, directed by Clyde Geromini (Disney, 1959).

At this point, I should acknowledge that linking love with nonviolence is far from inevitable in fiction. Many stories successfully combine love with heroic violence, and we can trace that pairing all the way back to antiquity. Consider Virgil's famous war epic, the *Aeneid*: Venus, the goddess of love, is the mother and patron of the titular warrior Aeneas. You don't get a more direct pairing of love and violence than that. (Well, technically the love affair of Aphrodite/Venus and Ares/Mars in classical mythology would be a more direct "pairing.")

On the other hand, some stories suffer from the disconnect between love and violence. Take the 2017 film *Wonder Woman*.[20] It features the Amazonian princess and demigod Diana who leaves home to become involved with the First World War. This ultimately leads to a confrontation with the god of War, Ares. Although a groundbreaking superhero film, some viewers were disappointed with the ending. Why is the third act of *Wonder Woman* merely serviceable, after two better acts?[21] I would argue this: by the climax, Diana functions as an avatar of love contra the god of war, Ares. Their violent duel, though, resonates better with war than love. This thematic disconnect is likely one reason the third act, although good enough to "land the plane," doesn't live up to the first two acts.[22]

Perhaps that's why the most iconic scene in the film is from the superior second act. This is the scene where we really see Diana becoming Wonder Woman. Determined to rescue an occupied town, Diana storms into the no man's land between trenches. She deflects bullets and mortar rounds with her vambraces and shield. Ultimately, she draws so much of the German's fire that the British troops are able to charge and overwhelm the German position. In this scene, her heroism isn't a matter of inflicting more violence than others could inflict, but rather of enduring more than others could endure. She is a shield rather than a sword. To be clear, Diana is by

---

[20] *Wonder Woman*, directed by Patty Jenkins (Warner Brothers, 2017).

[21] See Hanna Lodge's diagnosis of the film's third act problem in "Review: Wonder Woman Soars but Doesn't Stick the Landing," *The Beat*, May 30, 2017, https://www. comicsbeat.com/review-wonder-woman-soars/ (accessed September 24, 2024).

[22] The sequel *Wonder Woman 1984* (2020) suffers from a different problem: namely, not knowing how to structure a nonviolent campaign. Borrowing narrative structures from caper stories (and perhaps also detective stories) could have helped the second Wonder Woman adventure.

no means a pacifist figure here. She is still an active participant in a battle where enemies are slain. Nonetheless, there is still a better resonance with her symbolic role as an avatar of love.

Ultimately, a story driven by love has far greater potential for believable nonviolence than a story driven by hate. The task isn't to make violence impossible, but rather to make nonviolence possible. The subtle difference between the two is crucial. A love mythos doesn't guarantee or require nonviolent heroism in a story; it simply makes such heroism a lot easier to pull off.

Writing Exercise #11

A popular trope in romance fiction is "enemies to friends to lovers." This arc is also useful for thinking about social conflict narratives, even outside of the romance genre. Imagine, for example, a chemical plant polluting the groundwater in a working-class neighborhood. How might the locals and plant management move from enemies to friends? To help explore this scenario, sketch out answers to the following questions.

    a. How would the locals and the plant management view each other at the beginning of the story?

    b. What methods could the locals use to try to change the chemical plant's behavior?

    c. What setbacks/pushback might they encounter?

    d. What kind of crisis might compel the plant to change its behavior (bad publicity, disruptive protests, an accident at the plant, outside regulation, etc.)?

    e. What characters could drive this narrative? (For example, in an actual romance novel, you'd have the protagonist and antagonist begin on opposite sides of the conflict, but eventually fall in love.)

    f. How might an overarching love mythos help facilitate a happy ending?

Try running through these questions, or variants of them, with other scenarios of your own invention. Perhaps you'll find the seeds of a story.

Persuasion

Persuasion is the second cosmic power conducive to nonviolent heroism. Furthermore, we can find examples of persuasion as a cosmic force in both Eastern and Western religions. For the purpose of this book, we're not concerned with those religious concepts as matters of doctrine, but we'll consider how they can serve as models for mythos in fiction.

In his book *God and the World*, process theologian John Cobb, Jr. argued for persuasion rather than compulsion as the fundamental form of divine power. Compulsion, according to Cobb, depends upon the weakness of others and is a last resort after better methods of influence have failed. Persuasion, on the other hand, allows for "exercising power upon the powerful." Thus Cobb concluded, "The only power capable of any worthwhile result is the power of persuasion." For this reason, he favored an understanding of God as "The One Who Calls"—that is, a God who acts through divine persuasion.[23]

For a nontheistic parallel to Cobb's thought, consider chapter eight of the *Tao Te Ching* (traditionally attributed to Lao Tzu) which compares the *Tao* (or Way) to water. Rather than trying to elevate itself, water flows into low places. It doesn't try to guide or shape things, but simply finds a natural path. Yet water is beneficial in numerous ways and has a massive influence upon the world around it. For that reason, the *Tao Te Ching* offers water as both a metaphor for the *Tao* and a model for human leadership. Much like Cobb's God, the *Tao* is depicted as a cosmic force that acts through influence rather than coercion.[24]

If we engage Cobb and Lao Tzu on a narrative rather than dogmatic level, they help us identify certain possibilities for crafting imaginary worlds. Simply put, nonviolent heroism is much easier to pull off in a universe where persuasion rather than coercion is the fundamental form of cosmic power. When characters dig

---

[23]John B. Cobb, Jr., *God and the World* (Philadelphia: Westminster Press, 1969), 42, 89–90.

[24]Lao Tzu, *Tao Te Ching*, trans. A. S. Kline (Poetry in Translation, 2003), https://www.poetryintranslation.com/PITBR/Chinese/TaoTeChing.php (accessed September 24, 2024).

deeper, what will they find? The strength to coerce or the strength to persuade? The former will place us on the path toward violence far more quickly than the latter.

For a clear link between persuasion and nonviolence theory, we can turn to Quaker peace activist Vincent D. Nicholson, one of the founders of the American Friends Service Committee. He authored the very first Pendle Hill pamphlet, *Cooperation and Coercion as Methods of Social Change*, back in 1934. Both cooperation and coercion are strategies for resolving conflicts, according to Nicholson. The difference is that cooperation achieves through "education and persuasion ... the free-willing assent of both parties." Coercion, on the other hand, can only bring about "an outward compliance without an inner or free-willing assent." For this reason, cooperation is a more stable strategy for conflict resolution. Coercion doesn't truly resolve the root conflict, but merely suppresses it.[25]

Nicholson acknowledged, nonetheless, that not all forms of coercion are morally equal. He viewed war on the one hand and Gandhi's nonviolent boycott on the other hand as opposite extremes within the domain of coercion. Nicholson further acknowledged "that certain methods of coercion can be harmonized with the spirit of goodwill," and that the boundary between cooperation and coercion is sometimes blurry. Although he never quite formulated it, Nicholson was groping toward this critical question: Can a moral (nonviolent) method of coercion help us transition into a space where cooperation is possible?[26]

Three decades later, Martin Luther King, Jr. offered a powerful answer to that question in his famous "Letter from a Birmingham Jail." King's letter wasn't a direct response to Nicholson, but rather to a group of moderate clergy who had criticized civil rights demonstrations in Birmingham, Alabama. King responded by describing the city's history of persecuting Black citizens, as well as

---

[25]Vincent D. Nicholson, *Cooperation and Coercion as Methods of Social Change* (Wallingford, PA: Pendle Hill, 1934), 3.
[26]Ibid., 2–3, 11.

earlier, failed attempts to negotiate a solution. The protests, King argued, were necessary to create tension that would pressure the city leaders into good faith negotiations.[27]

King and Gandhi's activism walked the line between persuasion and coercion (at least as understood by Nicholson), but the rejection of violence meant they never entered a zone of pure coercion.[28] Gandhi sought to convert his oppressors, and King laid the groundwork for meaningful negotiations. Both goals align with persuasion. Of course, both activists had faith that they lived in a universe where nonviolent methods could prove effective.

The tension between coercion and persuasion may also play out in fictional worlds. For example, the short story "The Stubbornness of Wizards" by Eugene Morgulis, which first appeared in the final issue of *Fantasy Scroll Magazine*, places this tension at the core of its magic system.[29]

The central conflict of the story is between the wizard Grindleflog and a young girl named Dora who wants to be his student. He does everything he can to drive the girl away, while she stubbornly insists on being taught how to use her magical talent. We discover, though, that the two magic users have fundamentally different approaches to their craft. Grindleflog was trained in a coercive approach to magic. He demonstrates his power to Dora by causing a boulder to fly out of his garden. Then Grindleflog explains:

A wizard does not ask. A wizard commands. The rock may have wanted to stay put, but I wanted to see it fly. It is a matter of will, you see. Yours must be the strongest.[30]

---

[27]Martin Luther King, Jr., "Letter From Birmingham Jail," *Why We Can't Wait* (New York: Signet Books, 1964), 77–9. In his letter, King also described the self-discipline and training required for a nonviolent campaign.

[28]Different theorists favor different terms for this dichotomy. Cobb used "persuasion" versus "compulsion." Nicholson preferred "cooperation" versus "coercion." As for myself, I tend toward "persuasion" versus "coercion."

[29]Eugene Morgulis, "The Stubbornness of Wizards," *Fantasy Scroll Magazine* no. 13 (June 2016), 19–28.

[30]Ibid., 19.

The next day Grindleflog goes outside to discover Dora perched on that same boulder. She then explains how she convinced the boulder to return:

> It would not budge at first, but then I promised not to sit on it too long. Then the rock said ... 'Very well, but 300 years at the most.' And then it rolled here![31]

Grindleflog is scandalized. A true wizard doesn't negotiate, but rather commands. Nevertheless, Dora sticks with her approach to magic. Indeed, through an ongoing contest of wills with Grindleflog, her power of persuasion grows. The girl only leaves when she realizes that there's nothing more she can learn from the wizard, thus abandoning him to his self-imposed isolation. Ultimately, the path of coercion is a lonely one in this story. Conversely, when "Queen Theodora" appears in the story's epilogue, we grasp just how powerful persuasive magic can be. The new queen convinces an entire nation that monarchs should now be elected, and that they should furthermore choose her as their ruler. Even Grindleflog is won over by Queen Theodora, though he fails to recognize her as the girl from years before.

A magic system, however, is hardly a requirement for persuasion to operate as a mythic force. To the contrary, we find parallels even in realistic fiction. Jane Austen fans would no doubt protest if I overlooked her novel *Persuasion* while exploring this theme. In fact, two pivotal acts of persuasion set the novel's events in motion: 1) Lady Russell persuades her young friend Anne Elliot to break off her engagement with the penniless naval officer Captain Wentworth. 2) Nearly a decade later, the family lawyer persuades Anne's heavily indebted father, Sir Walter Elliot, to lease their manor to Admiral Croft, the brother-in-law of Captain Wentworth.[32]

This opening sets the tone for the novel as a whole, where the course of events is guided by a series of persuasive acts. Even when characters fail in their goals, these are often failures to persuade. For example, let's consider one of the scenes leading up to the leasing of the manor. The family lawyer, Mr. Shepherd, raises the idea of considering a naval officer for a tenant. At this point, three individuals make arguments to Sir Walter in favor of this

---

[31]Ibid., 20.
[32]Jane Austen, *Persuasion* (New York: Tor, 1999).

idea: Mr. Shepherd, his daughter Mrs. Clay, and Anne Elliot. Mr. Shepherd points out that naval officers are known to be generous with their money and therefore would likely agree to favorable terms. Mrs. Clay has always found sailors to be "neat and careful in all of their ways." Finally, Anne thinks that some consideration should be given to the navy's public service. Although Sir Walter isn't immediately won over, the conversation helps pave the way for the eventual arrangement with Admiral Croft.

Now I don't wish to downplay how patriarchy constrains Austen's protagonists, both in *Persuasion* and in her other novels. Austen did, however, intentionally locate the main action of her novels within spheres where her heroines had agency. War, violence, and coercion all exist in the universe of *Persuasion*, but they don't drive the central action. As the title suggests, persuasion is the crucial form of power. From the standpoint of mythos, Austen crafted a story world in which it is possible for persuasion rather than coercion to fill such a role.

In both of the examples above, coercion and persuasion coexist within the narrative world. Indeed, we're unlikely to find either pure persuasion or pure coercion in any given story, but the relative weight of these forces matters a great deal. On the one hand, in a story where the scales are tipped toward coercion, violent heroism will almost certainly carry the day. On the other hand, when a story tips toward persuasion, nonviolent heroism becomes a viable option. The more powerful persuasion becomes as a cosmic force in your fictional world, the easier it will be to imagine and depict credible, effective nonviolent action.

Writing Exercise #12

Think of a story that relies on violent coercion to solve the central conflict, such as a Western or action movie. Now imagine that the hero must rely on persuasion instead. Then sketch out answers to the following questions.

> a. What tactics could the hero attempt (appeals to reason, building alliances, mass protest, etc.)?

    b. What changes might the hero need to undergo before implementing such tactics?

    c. How would these shifts in both hero and tactics affect the main action of the story? What would that action look like? Where would it occur?

    d. How would you signal to your readers that persuasion is a credible option in your narrative universe?

Based on your answers to the questions above, try to outline or write a new story using original characters. Even if you never write a full version of the story, creating the outline may help you internalize strategies for depicting protagonists who act through persuasion. Try this experiment with different source materials to see which one inspires the most promising idea for a new story.

Reconciliation

Rather than a metaphysical exploration like the ones on "love" and "persuasion" above, let's begin this section by looking at the work that started me thinking about reconciliation in fiction, the cult classic movie *Robot Jox*. Now this is an objectively bad movie; although it falls into my "so bad it's good" category. The movie, which projects Cold War politics into a sci-fi future, faced box office doom when released into a world of collapsing Soviet power. Nonetheless, despite being saturated with the myth of redemptive violence, *Robot Jox* unexpectedly turns from revenge toward reconciliation in its final few minutes.

In the world of *Robot Jox*, war has been abolished following a devastating nuclear confrontation.[33] However, since the two global factions, Market and Confederacy (yes, capitalists and communists), can't be expected to refrain completely from fighting over territory, such disputes are settled through trial by combat—violent duels between faction champions driving giant robots.[34] These fights echo

---

[33]*Robot Jox*, directed by Stuart Gordan (Empire Pictures, 1990).
[34]These robots are commonly referred to as "mecha" in science fiction and anime circles.

the duel between Paris and Menelaus in the *Iliad* that would have settled the Trojan War, had the gods not interfered. This classical parallel was not lost on the filmmakers, who gave the gladiators names like Hercules, Achilles, and Athena.

The film culminates in a showdown over the fate of Alaska between Market champion Achilles and Confederacy champion Alexander—the latter an over-the-top, unhinged villain. Achilles wants revenge for the death of his friend Hercules, but he is looking forward to life after combat. Alexander, though, believes that gladiators must fight until they die. This fatalism inspires his cartoonishly evil persona. During the final fight sequence, highlights of which include space flight and a robot crotch chainsaw, both machines are disabled, and the warriors batter each other with pipes torn from their broken vehicles.

Achilles finally gains the upper hand and stands over the fallen Alexander. Unexpectedly, Achilles insists that they can both leave the field alive. Alexander disagrees, declaring, "We are dead. We are Robot Jox." Then Achilles throws away his pipe. Alexander stands up. He raises, then drops a large rock. The two share a conciliatory fist bump. The last frame of the movie, before the credits roll, is a close-up of the two fighters' techno-glove-encased fists. Although this ending is not entirely earned (if at all), it works because it has the same level of coherence as the rest of the film. Yet if this out-of-nowhere pivot in a somewhat disjointed story can provide a degree of audience satisfaction, what is possible when reconciliation is woven into the very fabric of a story's universe?

Before answering that question by exploring further examples, we must take a detour back into peace studies. For understanding the link between reconciliation and world building, let's consider the remarkable if controversial efforts of South Africa's post-apartheid Truth and Reconciliation Commission. For decades South Africa's government, controlled by the white minority, enforced a system of racial segregation and inequality called "apartheid." Anti-apartheid activism was brutally suppressed, and the state-controlled media prevented dissident voices from getting a fair hearing.

In the face of increasing pressures, including a global boycott movement in the 1980s, the South African government under F. W. de Klerk instituted a series of reforms in the early 1990s. This culminated in the dismantling of apartheid and a free election in 1994. Nelson Mandela, who had previously spent decades in prison for his anti-apartheid activism, was elected president, and de Klerk served as his vice president. The Truth and Reconciliation Commission from 1996 to 2003 allowed the new democracy to process its traumatic past.[35] It's important to acknowledge that the Truth and Reconciliation Commission has its critics. These charge that amnesty was granted too generously, whereas reparations for victims were too stingy.[36] With two decades of hindsight, scholars are ambivalent about its legacy, as both its strengths and weaknesses offer lessons for post-conflict peacebuilding. Even the critics, though, acknowledge that the Truth and Reconciliation Commission crafted a powerful narrative, and that is what concerns us in this chapter.

Tonya Goodman's *Staging Solidarity: Truth and Reconciliation in a New South Africa* offers a framework for understanding that work which resonates with literary analysis. Goodman described the Truth and Reconciliation Commission as "a space of storytelling and witnessing" and a "modern ritual of performance." It crafted victim testimonies into "a social drama of trauma and triumph" in the service of "a new national narrative."[37] "Storytelling," "performance," "drama," "narrative" are all terms one could also expect to find in a writing handbook.

According to Goodman, the Truth and Reconciliation Commission orchestrated several "cycles of performance." Or to put it another way, there were several layers of storytelling. The first layer came from the witness testimonies themselves. These provided an account of apartheid oppression, forcing the new democracy to reckon with the truth of the past. The second layer of storytelling came from the very structure of the hearings.[38] Goodman argued that these hearings were intentionally staged to create a sense of ritual drama. When victims first entered a hearing room to testify, the crowd rose to honor them. The commissioners then personally

---

[35]"South Africa," *Encyclopedia Britannica*, https://www.britannica.com/place/South-Africa (accessed September 19, 2021).

[36]Two books that raise these criticisms may be of particular interest to those exploring intersections between peace studies and literary studies: Wole Soyinka, *The Burden of Memory, the Muse of Forgiveness* (New York: Oxford University Press, 1999); Claire Moon, *Narrating Political Reconciliation: South Africa's Truth and Reconciliation Commission* (Lanham, MD: Lexington Books, 2009).

[37]Tanya Goodman, *Staging Solidarity: Truth and Reconciliation in a New South Africa* (Boulder, CO: Paradigm Publishers, 2009), 3.

[38]Ibid., 40–1.

greeted the victims and thanked them for coming. Following each person's testimony, one of the commissioners would respond with a summary—a way of validating to the witness that they had indeed been heard. These summaries also facilitated the process of weaving the individual statements into a collective master narrative.[39]

That master narrative was the third layer of storytelling, and it offered a vision of both past and future. The past was authoritarian, segregated, and traumatic. The future would be democratic, unified, and redemptive. Goodman even borrowed the terminology of pioneering sociologist Émile Durkheim to describe this difference: if the past was *profane*, the future was *sacred*.[40] Thus, the South African government, through the Truth and Reconciliation Commission, deliberately crafted a myth of reconciliation for their fledgling democracy.

It wasn't the South African government alone that communicated this mythos, though. Journalists had a key role in transmitting the story to local and global audiences. As such, the news media constituted a fourth layer of storytelling. Without widespread, sympathetic news coverage, it would have been much harder for the new mythos to take root. Finally, some of those audience members were inspired to create new artistic works based on the Truth and Reconciliation Commission and the story of apartheid, including films and literary works. These artistic creations constituted a fifth layer of storytelling.[41] Although now two decades in the past, South Africa's Truth and Reconciliation Commission serves as an influential real world case study in the synergy of myth, peacebuilding, and narrative art.

Just as South Africa's move toward reconciliation came at the end of the apartheid era, a work of fiction may move toward reconciliation near the story's end. In some cases, the protagonist may even be forced to choose between reconciliation, or at least forgiveness, and revenge. Consider Rebecca Burton's "The Choice" which appeared in the webzine *Abyss & Apex* in the summer of 2021.[42] In this story, the Egyptian goddesses Sekhmet visits a

---

[39] Ibid., 29, 45–71.

[40] Ibid., 30–1.

[41] Ibid., 40–1, 73–98.

[42] Rebecca Burton, "The Choice," *Abyss & Apex* no. 79 (June 4, 2021), https://www. abyssapexzine.com/2021/06/the-choice/ (accessed September 24, 2024).

woman whose heart and arm have recently been broken by a cruel lover. The goddess of retribution offers the woman vengeance and provides a vision of the violent tortures suffered by those within her power.

Ultimately, these tortures prove too vicious for the woman, despite her anger and pain. She rejects the proffered revenge, asking only 1) never to see the man again, and 2) that he be prevented from harming others. The goddess praises her for "choosing life" and promises to fulfill this request. The woman then asks what would have happened had she chosen the harsher option. The goddess explains, "Then you would have been judged, kitten, and found wanting, and your heart would never be healed."

In this story, it is actually forgiveness rather than reconciliation that has mythic power. Nonetheless, the two concepts are closely linked. Forgiveness is the necessary ground for reconciliation, but the former doesn't always require the latter. There's no reconciliation between the woman and her cruel lover, since he's out of her life for good, but forgiveness proves the first step in her internal healing process. Or to look at it from a different angle, she's able to reconcile with herself and re-engage with life.

In some works, there may be a split decision between reconciliation and revenge. For example, the main character may take revenge upon the antagonist while reconciling with a love interest. Even so, one or the other will probably prove more important for the story. Take William Shakespeare's *Much Ado About Nothing*, for example.[43] The young soldier Claudio is tricked by the villainous Don John into believing that his finance Hero has been unfaithful. As a result, Claudio publicly accuses and rejects Hero at their wedding ceremony the next day. This not only leads to estrangement between the lovers, but also between Claudio and his friend Benedict. The latter takes Hero's side and challenges Claudio to a duel.

If this were a tragedy like *Hamlet* or *Romeo and Juliet*, most of these characters would end up dead at the end. Since *Much Ado About Nothing* is a comedy, however, Hero merely fakes her own death. This turns out much better for her than it did for Juliet. When Don John's scheme is revealed, a penitent Claudio agrees to marry Hero's previously unknown "sister" concealed by a veil. When the

---

[43]William Shakespeare, "Much Ado about Nothing," *The Handy-Volume Shakespeare*, vol. 3 (New York: George Routledge and Sons, *c.* 1910), 4–111.

veil is lifted, Claudio's bride proves to be Hero herself. Benedict marries Hero's cousin Beatrice and reconciles with Claudio. Using Shakespeare's five acts, the arc could be summarized thus:

Act I. Claudio and Hero fall in love
Act II. Don John hatches his plan
Act III. Don John enacts his plan
Act IV. Estrangement
Act V. Reconciliation

The story builds toward reconciliation; this even decides its genre (comedy rather than tragedy). That is, the mythos of reconciliation determines what kind of story this is, what kind of universe the story takes place in, and what outcomes are possible in such a universe. With that said, there is still a gesture toward revenge at the end. A messenger announces that Don John has been captured, and Benedict promises to "devise thee brave punishments for him." That vague and perfunctory hint of vengeance, however, can hardly counterbalance the elaborate reconciliation plot. Reconciliation lies at the heart of the story. Revenge is merely an afterthought.

Some stories go further by rejecting revenge entirely, instead favoring reconciliation between the protagonist and antagonist. For stories emphasizing nonviolent heroism, this is an especially useful option. Such an ending can certainly serve the needs of serious drama, which is the path South Africa sought with the Truth and Reconciliation Commission. Even so, we're more likely to see this kind of ending in a comedy, perhaps due to the ancient distinction between comedies with happy endings and tragedies with sad endings.[44]

---

[44]On the ancient Greek stage, a "tragedy" was actually any serious drama. However, contra my own position, Aristotle considered tragedies with unhappy endings aesthetically superior to those with happy endings, and our English word "tragedy" traces its meaning to Aristotle's preference. From book 13 of *Poetics*: "In the second rank comes the kind of tragedy which some place first. Like the Odyssey, it has a double thread of plot, and also an opposite catastrophe for the good and for the bad. It is accounted the best because of the weakness of the spectators; for the poet is guided in what he writes by the wishes of his audience. The pleasure, however, thence derived is not the true tragic pleasure. It is proper rather to Comedy, where those who, in the piece, are the deadliest enemies—like Orestes and Aegisthus—quit the stage as friends at the close, and no one slays or is slain." S. H. Butcher, *Aristotle's Theory of Poetry and Fine Art: With a Critical Text and Translation of the Poetics*, 4th ed. with corrections (London: Macmillan and Co., 1911), 47–8.

The LEGO Movie provides us a good example.[45] In the film, an ordinary LEGO construction worker, Emmet, gets recruited to help stop the villainous Lord Business (also called President Business) from supergluing their entire world in place—along with all the inhabitants. The villain doesn't like how other people interfere with his vision of a perfect world. At the climax of the movie, Emmet confronts Lord Business. The latter appears to have the upper hand, but Emmet announces he has a secret weapon. When Lord Business pauses, Emmet holds out his hand in friendship. Emmet explains that what Lord Business sees as chaos, Emmet sees as inspiration. Lord Business, through his creations, has inspired others to find their own creativity.

By this point in the film, we've already discovered that the main story takes place in a world within a world. A young boy, Finn, has been playing with his father's elaborate LEGO scene, and the latter is ready to superglue his masterpiece in place to prevent further interference. The father is crushed, though, to realize that his LEGO doppelganger is the villain of his son's story. He begins to see things through Finn's eyes.

"If the construction guy said something to President Business, what would he say?" the father asks. Emmet then makes a speech about how Lord Business is a truly special and creative person. He wouldn't have to be the bad guy if he could just recognize that others can be special and creative as well. The hearts of both the father and Lord Business melt, and they simultaneously hug Finn and Emmet. Instead of the hero taking revenge on a defeated villain, the former antagonists reconcile.

There are some unexpected parallels to the end of apartheid in South Africa. Although Lord Business and the apartheid-era South African government both faced revolutionary activities, neither suffered a military defeat. In both cases, the established authorities voluntarily relinquished power after determining that their status quo was untenable. For this reason, revenge wasn't a viable endgame for either situation. In fact, taking revenge off the table was an explicit necessity in the South African negotiations.

Nor could the parties just go their separate ways, such as in Burton's "The Choice." Segregation—apartheid—had been a key source of injustice in the old South Africa. In the new South Africa,

---

[45]*The LEGO Movie*, directed by Christopher Miller and Phil Lord (Warner Brothers, 2014).

people of all races needed to find ways to coexist. The situation is similar in Emmet's LEGO world. Lord Business and his associates must live in—and reconcile with—the world they tried to freeze, a parallel to the father-son reconciliation in the movie's outer world.

This turn toward reconciliation is certainly easier in a comedy, where we're primed to look for happy endings. (Indeed, the resonance between comedy and nonviolence could be the topic of its own book.) Yet there is a path toward reconciliation even in serious tales. Some of the most profound tragedies, like *Romeo and Juliet* or the *Iliad*, reveal the humanity on both sides of a conflict. But pride, error, and mistrust prevent a peaceful resolution, and the narrative arc makes us believe that the destructive end is fated.[46]

According to Aristotle, the pity we feel when the inevitable doom descends can trigger a purging of emotions—a catharsis. But if pity can trigger catharsis, so can relief. Indeed, relief over reconciliation, I'm convinced, can be as powerful for an audience as pity over tragedy. The trick is to convince your audience that the characters are capable of heeding warnings, of learning, of changing in time—if fate and the gods will allow it.[47]

Writing Exercise #13

Re-read or think back to the old fairy tale of Hansel and Gretel, then answer the following questions.

   a. At the climax of the fairy tale, Gretel kills the witch. Come up with a nonviolent alternative. What happens instead?

   b. What common ground might the children and witch find? How could this help them reconcile?

---

[46]Shakespeare's opening description of Romeo and Juliet as "star-crossed lovers" alludes to astrology, and thus to fate. Aristotle addressed similarities between epic and tragedy at several points in *Poetics*. Certainly, the *Iliad* manifests tragedy in the thematic sense of the word.

[47]Aristotle, *Poetics*, books 6, 9 (Butcher, *Aristotle's Theory of Poetry and Fine Art*, 23, 39).

    c. What changes would you need to make earlier in the story, so that reconciliation becomes plausible?

    d. What is at stake for the characters in your revised version? Are the stakes still high enough to drive a compelling conflict? If not, how could you raise the stakes, while still leaving room for the eventual reconciliation?

Try this experiment with different fairy tales to see which one inspires the most promising idea for a new story. Fortunately, traditional fairy tales are public domain, so if you come up with a great adaptation, you can even publish it.

Conclusion

Is the universe "moral"? Does it have an "arc"—much less one that "bends toward justice"? These are questions of faith, not physics, so we all have to decide our own answers. Nor is this a new situation. Two millennia ago, Saint Paul urged his church in Philippi, "Work out your own salvation with fear and trembling" (Philippians 2:12).[48] I suspect many writers experience a similar sentiment when we sit down at our keyboards.

Nonetheless, a fictional story nearly always has an arc. The bend of that arc depends on choices made by the story's creator. What are the laws of the fictional universe? What kind of heroism can be effective given those laws? That is, what is the mythos of the fictional world? The mythos may be more obvious in fantastic worlds, but it is just as important for realistic worlds.

For guidance on how to facilitate nonviolent heroism in fictional worlds, we can consider those who accomplished the deed in our own world. That is, we can look toward activists who carried out successful nonviolent campaigns as examples. These activists consistently prioritized love over hate, persuasion over coercion, and reconciliation over revenge. By translating their ideals into cosmic forces, we can craft fictional worlds where nonviolent campaigns may plausibly triumph.

---

[48]Philippians 2:12; *The New Oxford Annotated Bible (New Revised Standard Version)*, 5th ed. (New York: Oxford University Press, 2018).

7

Peace Poetics for Activists

The primary focus of this book is on how to apply concepts from peace studies to the craft of fiction writing. In this chapter, however, we'll reverse the arrow of influence. That is, we'll look at how fiction writing skills and concepts can prove valuable to social justice activists.[1] To be honest, that could be the topic of its own book, and I'll just attempt an introductory foray here. The key thing to keep in mind, though, is that creative writing is a form of communication, and communication is an essential component of any social justice campaign. Thus, it shouldn't be surprising, in principle, if certain concepts resonate. Indeed, I've found two concepts especially valuable for thinking about how to move from peace poetics to practical activism: "creative literacy" and "counternarrative." I'll explain both below, but let's begin by looking at "creative literacy."

Creative Literacy

The term "creative literacy" as used in the field of creative writing studies[2] was coined by poet and English professor Steve Healey. In a 2009 article for *The Writer's Chronicle*, Healey addressed a seeming paradox: creative writing programs were increasing in popularity,

---

[1]Portions of this chapter first appeared in the article "Narratology and Narrative Change" in the Spring 2022 issue of *The Peace Chronicle*.

[2]Beyond creative writing studies, the term "creative literacy" is sometimes used by primary and secondary educators to refer to creative approaches to literacy education. That sense of "creative literacy," while valuable in its own right, falls outside the focus of this book.

while the types of literature they taught students to write (namely, poetry and short fiction) were decreasing in popularity. Why were students gravitating toward a field that was apparently losing value? Healey argued that the creative skills learned through these courses were actually of great value in the knowledge economy, but they were being put to different uses than writing instructors anticipated.[3] Instead of writing the next great novel, for example, a former creative writing student might work on the next big ad campaign. While that may seem dispiritingly commercial, just remember that creative messaging is as important for human rights organizations as it is for sneaker brands. If peace poetics proves useful for activists, this utility may manifest in types of writing that aren't purely artistic.

Indeed, Healey argued that there is no zone of pure creativity, external to our socio-economic structures, for artists to retreat into. Therefore, it's imperative to think about what it means to act ethically as a creative person within those structures. Drawing on Richard Florida's *The Rise of the Creative Class*, and noting the rise of "creativity" as a buzzword in business programs, Healey used the term "creative literacy" to describe the portable skills one could learn in a creative writing course. Healey was not, however, a naive cheerleader for late capitalism or the status quo. He warned that the "privatization of creativity can have dangerous effects, including the undermining of public dissent that's often associated with artistic activity." For creative writing instructors to teach their students about these dangers, though, requires a clear vision of how creativity functions in the modern marketplace.[4]

---

[3]Steve Healey, "The Rise of Creative Writing & the New Value of Creativity," *The Writer's Chronicle*, February 2009. The *Writer's Chronicle* archive where I found this article was taken offline by its publisher before this book went to print. Fortunately, Healey repurposed the article as "Movement 1.0 Thinking Outside Creative Writing" in his 2009 doctoral dissertation, *The Rise of Creative Writing and the New Value of Creativity*, University of Minnesota, https://conservancy.umn.edu/server/api/core/bitstreams/23aee473-97db-439b-82db-6cd2eee40d0e/content (accessed October 4, 2024).

[4]Ibid. Although she didn't use the term "creative literacy," Stephanie Vanderslice offered a similar perspective when she insisted that her job was to empower creative writing students "to make a creative living in some way with words," even if most wouldn't become published authors. *Rethinking Creative Writing in Higher Education: Programs and Practices that Work* (Wicken, UK: The Professional and Higher Partnership, 2011), 26–7.

Healey further explored the concept of creative literacy in a pair of book chapters from 2013 and 2015.[5] In "Beyond the Literary: Why Creative Literacy Matters," he described the "many proficiencies" that creative literacy develops, including the use of language "to produce complex affective states in an audience" and "the ability to manipulate or destabilize received meanings and produce new meanings."[6] Both of these are also applicable to social activism, as we can see by considering the American Civil Rights Movement in the 1960s. Certainly, Martin Luther King, Jr.'s "I Have a Dream" speech has proven its ability to "produce complex affective states in an audience." Indeed, its power to affect people emotionally has made the speech an enduring classic. As for the dismantling of Jim Crow in the US South, that required nothing less than to "destabilize received meanings and produce new meanings." Ending segregation and expanding voting rights involved replacing one understanding of how society should be ordered with a new understanding.

Now, I'm certainly not claiming that the Civil Rights Movement can be reduced to a form of creative writing. That would be absurd! However, I do believe those civil rights activists made use of many of the skills that Healey included under the umbrella of "creative literacy." Furthermore, the purpose of peace poetics is to facilitate a form of storytelling compatible with social justice and peace efforts. As an approach to creative writing, peace poetics can help students, writers, and activists develop their creative literacy—and it does so in a manner that is innately in sync with social justice activism.

In "Creative Literacy Pedagogy," Healey explored another useful aspect of this topic: presentation. He pointed out that print publication is the traditional way of presenting a piece of creative writing. However, if we think of creative products more broadly (as we must if we take creative literacy seriously), such products could be presented in any number of ways. Just consider the range of how creative work might be presented within a civil rights campaign. Options include political speeches, social media campaigns, and

---

[5]Steve Healey, "Beyond the Literary: Why Creative Literacy Matters," *Key Issues in Creative Writing*, ed. Dianne Donnely and Graeme Harper (Bristol, UK: Multilingual Matters, 2013), 48–78. Steve Healey, "Creative Literacy Pedagogy," *Creative Writing Pedagogies for the Twenty-First Century*, ed. Alexandria Peary and Tom C. Hunley (Carbondale, IL: Southern Illinois University Press, 2015), 169–93.
[6]Healey, "Beyond the Literary," 63.

even imaginative street protests. Healey's pedagogy deliberately prepared his students to apply creativity to tasks that went beyond traditional forms of creative writing. He asked them to imagine various ways their work could be presented, and even incorporated these alternative settings and purposes into the writing prompts for class assignments. While his assignments weren't necessarily focused on social justice issues, they did prepare students to apply their creative skills in diverse ways.[7]

Healey's concept of creative literacy helps us understand how peace poetics could prove useful *in principle* to peace and justice activists. I haven't shown, though, that peace poetics is useful for activists *in practice*. We can certainly imagine how this might prove true. Understanding the narrative structure of civil resistance campaigns could allow activists to communicate more effectively about their activities. A deeper understanding of character arcs and conflict transformation theory might help them see past seemingly frozen states of polarization to future possibilities for conversion and cooperation. Finally, if activists understood what "mythic forces" make a better world conceivable, they could cultivate and propagate a worldview rooted in those forces. This claim doesn't depend on a specific set of metaphysical beliefs. It merely assumes that ideas influence human actions and therefore how we live in the world. But we can do more than just imagine the possible impact of peace poetics, as literary concepts are already influencing the field of social justice activism. One of the most important of these concepts is "counternarrative."

Counternarrative

In the essay "counternarrative" for their book *Writing Intersectional Identities: Keywords for Creative Writers*, Janelle Adsit and Renée M. Byrd discussed several terms coined by different writers for the same basic concept: "grand narrative" from Jean-François Lyotard, "master narrative" from Toni Morrison, and "single story" from Chimamanda Ngozi Adichie. All of these terms indicate how

---

[7]Healey, "Creative Literacy Pedagogy," 186–9.

dominant cultural perspectives take on narrative form. If cultural narratives tell stories about how things are and why, dominant narratives can overpower alternative stories.[8]

The narrative of Manifest Destiny, for example, tells a tale of heroically taming an empty wilderness.[9] If you found yourself putting mental scare quotes around "heroic," "taming," and "empty," then you have started to intuit the power and danger of dominant narratives. The Manifest Destiny narrative served to render invisible the cultures of indigenous peoples, or else to cast them as "savages" in a tale that had no room for their authentic experiences. This is hardly a new indictment. We're now a half-century past the publication of N. Scott Momaday's *The Way to Rainy Mountain*—a blend of history, folklore, and memoir that served as both tribute and elegy for his Kiowa ancestors.[10] Through Momaday's voice and others, the cost of this particular dominant narrative has long since been exposed.

Adsit and Byrd asked writers to think about the following question: "What stories are you reinforcing when you write?"[11] The point of this question wasn't to stifle writers, but to invite us to think about a wider range of story possibilities, and to be deliberate about what narratives we challenge or support. Peace poetics strives to do this. Its purpose is to create counternarratives to the "myth of redemptive violence" (to bring back Walter Wink's phrase from before). Thus, if the concept of "counternarrative" proves useful to activists, then peace poetics offers tools for crafting a particular subset of counternarratives. This is important because counternarratives are already being used as the foundation for certain types of social justice campaigns.

One organization that has done significant work in designing and theorizing campaigns built around counternarratives is Narrative Initiative, a project of the New Venture Fund. Its purpose is "to make equity and social justice common sense" by challenging dominant narratives that undermine progressive efforts. Narrative

---

[8]Janelle Adsit and Renée M. Byrd, *Writing Intersectional Identities: Keywords for Creative Writers* (New York: Bloomsbury Academic, 2019), 73–9.

[9]Ibid., 73.

[10]N. Scott Momaday, *The Way to Rainy Mountain* (Albuquerque, NM: University of New Mexico Press, 1969).

[11]Adsit and Byrd, *Writing Intersectional Identities*, 78.

Initiative refers to this process as "narrative change." Its focus is on facilitating and assisting long-term social justice campaigns that challenge harmful dominant narratives by offering powerful counternarratives.[12]

Narrative Initiative has made significant contributions toward systematizing a vocabulary for narrative change work. A key concept is the distinction between "story" and "narrative." These words are near synonyms in everyday English, but they have technical meanings within the field of narrative change. (These are different from the definitions of "story" and "narrative" used in narratology, but we'll address that discrepancy later in the chapter.) A "story" is a specific literary work or any other discrete manifestation of a tale. Structurally (as Aristotle long ago observed) a story has a beginning, middle, and end. A "narrative" is a collection of similar stories that reinforce each other. If the Broadway musical *West Side Story* is a story, then "doomed love" is an underlying narrative. This narrative is certainly older than *West Side Story*, or Shakespeare's *Romeo and Juliet* which inspired the musical. It's even older than the tragic romance of Dido and Aeneas in Virgil's *Aeneid*. "Doomed love" is a narrative encompassing a large number of stories. Certain narratives are especially powerful. The term "deep narrative" defines a pervasive and intractable narrative that is fundamental to a person or culture's worldview.[13] For example, the film *How the West Was Won* is a story that reflects the deep narrative of Manifest Destiny.

FrameWorks and the Bootstraps Narrative

Another major player in the field of narrative change is the FrameWorks Institute. They describe themselves as "a think tank that helps mission-driven organizations communicate about

---

[12] "About Us," Narrative Initiative, https://narrativeinitiative.org/about-us/ (accessed October 31, 2022).

[13] "Narrative Change: A Working Definition (and Some Related Terms)," Narrative Initiative, May 15, 2019, https://narrativeinitiative.org/blog/narrative-change-a-working-definition-and-related-terms/ (accessed September 24, 2024).

social issues in ways that build public will to support progressive change." FrameWorks has developed a concept called "Strategic Frame Analysis" that provides a social scientific foundation for counternarrative campaigns.[14] As they explain it, "A frame is a guide. It directs people where to look, but more importantly, helps them interpret what they see." Activists need to make deliberate choices about how they frame their messages to have maximum impact on an audience. Frameworks has identified over a dozen "frame elements," including context, explanatory metaphors, messengers, and narrative.[15]

Given the topic of this book, the FrameWorks Institute understanding of narrative is especially relevant. FrameWorks builds off the work of Narrative Initiative, but they diverge in one important way. According to FrameWorks, a narrative is not only a collection of related stories, but also the underlying pattern shared by those stories. There's a "chicken or egg" relationship between stories and narratives. Although a narrative may initially emerge from a collection of disparate stories, it eventually becomes a template for new stories that reinforce the narrative.[16]

FrameWorks developed these ideas in a 2021 report entitled "The Features of Narrative: A Model of Narrative Form for Social Change Efforts." A notable feature of this report is the influence of literary theory. I have on my bookshelf a copy of *The Norton Introduction to Literature* by Kelly J. Mays, a book I once used to teach a literature-based composition course.[17] Several of the fundamental topics from that book also appear in the FrameWorks report, including character, plot, setting, and point of view. This runs counter to perceptions of English as an "impractical"

---

[14]"About Us," FrameWorks Institute, https://www.frameworksinstitute.org/about/ (accessed November 11, 2022).

[15]"What's in a Frame?" FrameWorks Institute, July 16, 2020, https://www.frameworksinstitute.org/article/whats-in-a-frame/ (accessed September 24, 2024).

[16]"The Features of Narrative: A Model of Narrative Form for Social Change Efforts," FrameWorks Institute, September 2021, 7, https://www.frameworksinstitute.org/wp-content/uploads/2021/09/The-features-of-narratives.pdf (accessed September 24, 2024).

[17]Kelly J. Mays, *The Norton Introduction to Literature, Shorter*, 12th ed. (New York: W. W. Norton, 2016).

discipline. As it turns out, even introductory literary concepts have real world utility.[18]

As an example, we can look at "character" and "plot" in the "bootstraps narrative." In this dominant narrative, a driven but down-on-their-luck protagonist (character) overcomes the odds and achieves great success through their own hard work and determination (plot).[19] Take the story of Chris Gardner in *The Pursuit of Happyness*. Gardner was a homeless, single father who persevered in a competitive Wall Street internship. This put him on the path toward becoming a millionaire.[20]

In the case of Gardner, this was a true story. Part of what makes the bootstraps narrative powerful is that sometimes it does play out in real life. However, it isn't scalable. This narrative inevitably leaves a lot of people behind, since there's not enough room for everyone at the top of the pyramid. There's no place in the bootstraps narrative for the many, many people who work hard without getting ahead.

Furthermore, the narrative gets misapplied to those who achieve success, but also start out with important advantages, such as social connections and inherited wealth. An exchange in the movie *Get Hard* satirizes this tendency.[21] The finance titan Martin declares to his right-hand man, "I built this company with my two own hands. Just me, that computer, and an eight million dollar loan from my father." His lieutenant replies, "You really did it all on your own." By the end of the movie, though, *Get Hard* undermines the bootstraps narrative and offers instead a powerful counternarrative—that everyone needs a helping hand.

Intriguingly, we can also find the "helping hand" counternarrative represented in Will Smith's long acting career. In the episode "Will Gets a Job" from *The Fresh Prince of Bel-Air*,[22] Will explains to his Uncle Phil that he got a restaurant job to be self-reliant, just like his uncle. Uncle Phil, though, rejects that characterization. He

---

[18]"Features of Narrative," FrameWorks, 17–22.

[19]Ibid., 26.

[20]These details are common both to Gardner's autobiography and the biopic starring Will Smith. I'll admit, I'm only directly familiar with the latter: *The Pursuit of Happyness*, directed by Gabriele Muccino (Columbia Pictures, 2006).

[21]*Get Hard*, directed by Etan Cohen (Warner Brothers, 2015).

[22]"Will Gets a Job," directed by Ellen Gittlesohn, *The Fresh Prince of Bel-Air* (The Stuffed Dog Company, 1991).

insists, "Nobody does anything without help, Will. People opened doors for me, and I've worked hard to open doors for you. It doesn't make you any less of a man to walk through them."

FrameWorks Institute, however, doesn't reject the bootstraps narrative outright. They instead suggest a way it could be redirected. To do this, they make a distinction between the bootstraps narrative and the narrative of meritocracy. The latter assumes equality of opportunity, whereas the former acknowledges that some people may start with a disadvantage. Thus, FrameWorks asks, "Could the bootstraps narrative be tweaked and redirected as a narrative about resistance to unfair systems—how individuals can, through determination and force of will, change the systems that constrain their communities?"[23] If so, peace poetics certainly offers valuable tools for crafting such stories of resistance.

Narratology and Narrative Change

At this point, we need to consider more closely some of the terminology used in narrative change work. It's common for specialized fields to take terms from ordinary language and give them narrow, technical meanings. This redefinition doesn't suddenly invalidate how the "person on the street" uses the word, of course. The broader meaning still applies in everyday life. The new, technical meaning simply serves the needs of that specialized field. Sometimes, words that are near-synonyms in everyday language take on important distinctions in particular fields.

It's also possible, though, for different fields to give different technical meanings to the same term. Neither field is wrong; both are responding to their particular needs. But what if two such fields might benefit from cross-fertilization? What if ideas from one field may prove beneficial to the other? If those fields are using the same words in different ways, such cross-fertilization requires a translation key.

This is the situation, I believe, for the fields of narratology and narrative change work. The former field has studied narrative form

---

[23]"Features of Narrative," FrameWorks, 33.

and function for over fifty years. It would be quite surprising if none of narratology's insights were applicable to narrative change work! However, the key terms "story" and "narrative" are used differently in the two fields, hence the need for translation.[24] Let's first look at some relevant terms from narratology, although these are brief and simplified definitions:

- Story: The events that happen in a tale in their chronological order. (In the early twentieth century, the Russian formalists used the word *fabula* to describe this, and some theorists still prefer the Russian term.)

- Discourse: How a tale is told. For example, events may be told out of order, or in differing degrees of detail. (In the early twentieth century, the Russian formalists used the word *syuzhet* to describe this, and some theorists still prefer the Russian term.)

- Narrative: The combination of story and discourse that constitute a distinct tale or literary work.

We can also use the following definitions from narrative change work:

- Story: A work in any medium (textual, visual, or oral) that follows a plot arc and portrays specific characters and events.

- Narrative: A story pattern or story template that is pervasive in a culture. Individual stories may fully or partially reflect/reinforce a dominant narrative.

- Narrative change: A long-term effort to shift a dominant cultural narrative toward one more compatible with a social cause.

In both cases, "narrative" represents a higher order concept, and "story" represents a lower order concept. However, the two fields are offset from each other. Narratology uses the term "narrative"

---

[24]Seymour Chatman's *Story and Discourse: Narrative Structure in Fiction and Film* (Ithaca, NY: Cornell University Press, 1978) has exerted a great influence over the terminology used in English language narratology.

to describe the discrete literary works that are called "stories" in narrative change work. Narratology doesn't have a term for the higher order concept that narrative change work designates "narrative." On the other hand, the narrative change field lacks terms for the lower order concepts that narratology designates "story" and "discourse." The following proposed translation key fills in these missing blanks.

Narratology		Narrative Change
myth		narrative
narrative		story
story		*content*
discourse		*form*

I've italicized my additions in the above chart. Basically, I'm proposing that we use "myth" or "mythos" in narratology to describe what the narrative change field calls "narrative." And we can use the terms "content" and "form" as the narrative change equivalents of "story" and "discourse." With the above key in mind, theorists from one field can read work in the other field, while keeping track of what the common words mean. Just as importantly, theorists can import concepts from one field to the other without confusing readers in their primary field. Admittedly, this is a somewhat clunky solution, but it should work.[25]

If peace poetics does develop as a field, it might even take the lead in pursuing such translation work. After all, bridging the gap between narratology and narrative change could also open up new possibilities for creative writing. In an earlier chapter, we explored how to harmonize the structure of confidence tales with the structure of civil resistance campaigns, but that's just a useful starting point. Different counternarratives will likely call for different structures. By identifying which genres might be utilized or transformed to serve particular counternarrative campaigns, peace poetics could make valuable contributions to social justice activism.

---

[25]It's important to note that the vocabularies of both fields are much richer than what I've included here. My main purpose has been to address a particular source of potential confusion. Perhaps this modest effort, though, will help facilitate greater exchange between these fields.

Conclusion

It may be a bit jarring to think about repurposing the creative writing toolbox for social or political causes. After all, a certain school of thought insists that literature should always be apolitical, that rhetorical intentions are innately aesthetic sins. Politics and rhetoric, though, aren't so easy to escape. In his book *Workshops of Empire: Stegner, Engle, and American Creative Writing during the Cold War*, Eric Bennett convincingly demonstrated that this doctrine of literary neutrality—or at least, the version of it that has proliferated in American creative writing MFA programs—is itself a product of Cold War-era politics. By de-emphasizing social causes in favor of individual psychology, American literature formed a bulwark against Soviet collectivism.[26] But as sometimes happens, this aesthetic dogma has outlived its original conditions.

Now, the dogma isn't entirely wrong. If we view creative literature simply as politics by other means, then we lose sight of fiction's unique *literary* virtues. Fiction can create room for multiple perspectives, leaving space (at least sometimes) for readers to make up their own minds. This capacity for ambivalence is a gift in fiction, not a weakness. We would impoverish literature if we treated it as nothing more than a specialized form of argumentation.

However, the aesthetic dogma crosses the line when it entirely prohibits political and rhetorical motives. In this I'm guided by Alfred North Whitehead's warning from *Religion in the Making*:

A dogma may be true in the sense that it expresses such interrelations of the subject matter as are expressible within the set of ideas employed. But if the same dogma be used intolerantly so as to check the employment of other modes of analyzing the subject matter, then, for all its truth, it will be doing the work of falsehood.[27]

---

[26]Eric Bennett, *Workshops of Empire: Stegner, Engle, and American Creative Writing during the Cold War* (Iowa City, IA: University of Iowa Press, 2015).
[27]Alfred North Whitehead, *Religion in the Making* (New York: The Macmillan Company, 1926), 131.

It may be true that art should exist for art's sake, but that truth shouldn't be used to exclude every *other* purpose an artwork might have. The novelist Margaret Atwood had something interesting to say about this in her Substack newsletter. She asked the question "what is a novel?" The answers ranged from "A) A political tract" to "F) A work of art." Atwood then insisted, "The correct answer is F), though a novel may CONTAIN any and all of these other things."[28] Here Atwood captured the balance between emphasizing one truth and leaving room for other truths. The first clause of her sentence clarified what is true in the aesthetic dogma; the second clause prevented the dogma from "doing the work of a falsehood." Art must be aesthetic or else it isn't art, but art might also be social or political.

Of course, it's one thing to say that a novel may contain a political tract. It's another thing to say that the creative writer's toolbox can be repurposed for writing political tracts, or for crafting social media campaigns, or for weaving counternarratives into public discourse through diverse genres and media. Yet the notion of creative literacy asks us to at least consider the latter possibility. Ultimately, the boundaries between creative texts and other forms of discourse are permeable. Because of this, ideas and skills from the world of creative literature can benefit peace and justice activists in many ways.

---

[28]Margaret Atwood, "Some Very Basic Basics About Writing Novels," *In the Writing Burrow*, November 22, 2022, https://margaretatwood.substack.com/p/some-very-basic-basics-about-writing (accessed September 24, 2024).

8

Conclusion

There is very little left to do in this book, or perhaps much more than can be done. The great challenge of any book is determining what will fit between the covers. It's always possible to dig deeper or stretch further. But a book must end; some things must wait for other books. In that spirit, I've accomplished nearly all of the essential tasks for this present text. I've laid out my core ideas regarding the craft of pacifist fiction, and I've even hinted at how such work may be of value to peace and justice activists. That only leaves three remaining tasks for this brief conclusion: 1) to indicate some future possibilities for peace poetics, 2) to warn against excessive purity or literalism in applying the ideas in this book, and 3) to consider how the ideas from various chapters fit together.

Future Directions for Peace Poetics

Let's now consider some future directions for peace poetics. The list that follows is hardly comprehensive; it just includes several of my own ideas that didn't fit within the scope of this project. I may write more on these in the future, or perhaps they'll prove a springboard for someone else's work.

- The chapter on character arcs uses conflict resolution theory to analyze characters in fiction, and even includes suggestions for future work along that line. This is far from the only possible approach to character construction, though. Peace psychology offers another valuable resource. In particular

Marshall Rosenberg's *Nonviolent Communication* and V. K. Kool and Rita Agrawal's *Gandhi and the Psychology of Nonviolence* offer new ways to think about dialogue, motivation, and other character-related issues.[1]

- This book has relied heavily on Western approaches to peace and conflict studies (the work of Gandhi being the major exception). That's due in no small part to how and where I was trained. However, as Victoria Fontan and others have pointed out, this can result in perception gaps.[2] Other parts of the world have their own conflict resolution systems, and some of these go back centuries. I have no doubt that these peace traditions also offer fertile storytelling resources.

- This book has also leaned heavily on Western plot structures, such as the three-act structure favored by Syd Field.[3] That is hardly the only possible form of plot. Consider *kishotenketsu*, the four-act structure common in East Asian writing: introduction, development, twist, conclusion.[4] We could certainly map a nonviolent campaign onto that plot structure, and it would allow us to pace the story differently. Furthermore, Jane Alison's *Meander, Spiral, Explode* maps out a range of alternative plot structures.[5] Exploring all of these is beyond the scope of this book, so it's a fertile area for future work.

---

[1]Marshall B. Rosenberg, *Nonviolent Communication: A Language of Life*, 3rd ed. (Encinitas, CA: PuddleDancer Press, 2015). V. K. Kool and Rita Agrawal, *Gandhi and the Psychology of Nonviolence*, vol. 1: *Scientific Roots and Development*; vol. 2: *Applications Across Psychological Science* (Cham, Switzerland: Palgrave Macmillan, 2020).

[2]Victoria Fontan, *Decolonizing Peace* (Lake Oswego, OR: Dignity Press, 2012).

[3]Syd Field, *The Screenwriter's Workbook* (New York: Dell Publishing, 1984).

[4]English language resources on this topic are somewhat limited. For a brief but scholarly treatment, see Joann Temple Dennett, "Not to Say is Better Than to Say: How Rhetorical Structure Reflects Cultural Context in Japanese-English Technical Writing," *IEEE Transactions on Professional Communication* 31, no. 3 (September 1998), 116–19. For a more general treatment that emphasizes narrative, see the TV Tropes article on "kishotenketsu," https://tvtropes.org/pmwiki/pmwiki.php/Main/Kishotenketsu (accessed September 24, 2021)

[5]Jane Alison, *Meander, Spiral, Explode: Design and Pattern in Narrative* (New York: Catapult, 2019).

- Although Aristotle emphasized tragedy, comedy may be the more potent genre for nonviolent heroism. That's because both comedy and nonviolence have a subversive dimension. They undermine the status quo in order to imagine different possibilities. Comedy can certainly be violent, as the Tom and Jerry cartoons show, but there is still resonance and potential synergy between comedy and nonviolence.

- We have become increasingly aware that peace, justice, and ecology are intertwined. The United States Pentagon even considers climate change a national security issue.[6] As such, ecocriticism may prove a useful resource for peace poetics by indicating diverse ways to integrate an ecological perspective into writing.

I suspect (and hope) that you'll come up with other ideas on your own. That would allow peace poetics to grow into a field. Eventually, perhaps, someone will even write a dense, academic monograph on the topic. As a book nerd, that's a work I'd enthusiastically read. Even so, I also hope that the aims of this present book aren't forgotten. However dense or theoretical particular works may become, peace poetics must always, ultimately, arc back around to the practical needs of writers. That's what I've tried to do here.

Against Purity

I also should warn against pacifist purity, at least in fiction writing. Indeed, I recognize how my keen championing of peace and nonviolence might tempt one toward excessive purity. But as a fiction writer myself, I also realize that there's no such thing as a perfect story, and part of how we finish our work is by deciding what compromises to make. As the literary critic Wayne C. Booth observed, "all authors are disloyal, at one point or another, to the

---

6Lloyd J. Austin, III, "Statement by Secretary of Defense Lloyd J. Austin III on Tackling the Climate Crisis at Home and Abroad," US Department of Defense, January 27, 2021, https://www.defense.gov/News/Releases/Release/Article/2484504/statement-by-secretary-of-defense-lloyd-j-austin-iii-on-tackling-the-climate-cr/ (accessed September 24, 2024).

general standards they profess; they have to be if they are to take *this* intractable work ... from page one to page the last."[7]

Is there a role for heroic violence (as opposed to villainous violence) in works of "nonviolent" fiction? This question parallels, to some extent, one that Erica Chenoweth asked in *Civil Resistance: What Everyone Needs to Know*: "Is it fair to expect oppressed people to fight back against oppression using only civil resistance?" Chenoweth emphatically answered, "No." She noted that even Mahatma Gandhi preferred violence to cowardice, and also cited the pacifist activist Bill Sutherland, who distinguished between *his own* convictions and choices and the expectations he placed on *others*.[8]

Now Chenoweth, Gandhi, and Sutherland all embraced nonviolent resistance on both practical and ethical grounds. Furthermore, the latter two also embraced nonviolence on metaphysical grounds. Yet all three recognized the danger of projecting a strict purity code onto other activists, and I must offer a similar warning with regard to fiction. It's better to write a mostly nonviolent story that works than a purely nonviolent story that fails. What kind of violent heroism, then, might be compatible with a mostly nonviolent story? A few possibilities occur to me:

1. The protagonists attempt heroic violence, but this proves futile or counterproductive. Thus, they must find alternatives.

2. The heroic violence is effective, but insufficient. Although violent heroism exists, the most important heroic acts are nonviolent.

3. The acts of heroic violence occur in the earlier parts of the story, and thus reflect the protagonist's incomplete growth arc. This could be paired with either of the two above.

4. The story builds toward ambivalence over violent methods. Both violence and nonviolence accomplish something significant, allowing for a divided jury regarding the utility of violence.

---

[7] Wayne C. Booth, *The Rhetoric of Fiction*, 2nd ed. (University of Chicago Press, 1983), 9.

[8] Erica Chenoweth, *Civil Resistance: What Everyone Needs to Know* (New York: Oxford University Press, 2021), 78–80.

If your attempts to craft nonviolent heroism feel too tidy, allow some messiness in. There's room for your protagonists to act out, make mistakes and wrong choices, or just experiment with different methods. If they are the right characters in the right world, their growth arcs will carry them back to nonviolence in the end.

Fitting Things Together

Finally, I should give some consideration to how the ideas from various chapters fit together. Let's look again at the Bollywood musical *Lage Raho Munna Bhai*.[9] We discussed this movie in the chapter on campaigns, but it could also have factored into our discussions of character arcs and world building. Munna Bhai certainly goes through a growth arc where he has to abandon the Lie and embrace the Truth. This even takes on literal form when he must confess the truth about his background. This initially costs the reformed gangster the love of his life, but it's a necessary part of his path.

Furthermore, in the world of the movie, love and reconciliation prove to be more powerful forces than greed and ruthlessness. This is shown in how Munna Bhai finally saves the nursing home. Lucky Singh's motivation for seizing the property is to give his daughter a home as a wedding gift. Munna Bhai approaches the young woman at her wedding and reveals how her father obtained the house. She is horrified at how the elderly residents were treated, leading to the alienation of father from daughter. However, Munna Bhai then intercedes on Lucky Singh's behalf. He explains to the new bride that her father's actions, though dastardly, were rooted in his love for her. The reconciliation with his daughter melts Lucky Singh's heart, and he gratefully hands over the deed to the nursing home. Altogether, the main character has a growth arc that allows him to successfully wage a nonviolent campaign in a universe where such things are possible.

The example of *Munna Bhai* shows that the strategies outlined in different chapters can be layered on top of each other. The main

---

[9]*Lage Raho Munna Bhai*, directed by Rajkumar Hirani (Vinod Chopra Productions, 2006).

character's growth arc can be synchronized to the unfolding of a civil resistance campaign. A duel scene can be incorporated wherever the story needs an extra jolt, such as a key turning point or the climax, with the violence subverted by whichever approach best fits the story.[10] The efficiency of love, persuasion, and reconciliation can be woven into the fabric of the narrative universe, allowing for the campaign's eventual success.

With that said, not every tool or idea needs to be used in every story. In your future projects, some chapters from this book may prove more important than others. You may even find yourself using ideas from this book in stories that aren't meant to be pacifist or nonviolent. That's all for the good. After all, I'm seeking greater balance, not the abolition of violent storytelling. The more these tools are adopted, the more widely alternatives to violence will circulate, and the easier it will become to imagine peace.

---

[10]The film's most obvious "duel" doesn't illustrate one of the specific strategies I proposed in the duel chapter, but it's worth noting, nonetheless. There's fight scene in which Munna Bhai gives up too easily on "turning the other cheek," thus illustrating his need for further growth.

BIBLIOGRAPHY

Note: Certain works mentioned in passing in the main text have been omitted from this bibliography. In many cases, citations for these works are provided in the footnotes.

"The Abandoned Princess," *The Columbia Anthology of Traditional Korean Poetry*, edited by Peter H. Lee (New York: Columbia University Press, 2002), 298–29.

"About Us." FrameWorks Institute. https://www.frameworksinstitute.org/about/ (accessed November 11, 2022).

"About Us." Narrative Initiative. https://narrativeinitiative.org/about-us/ (accessed October 31, 2022).

Adsit, Janelle and Renée M. Byrd. *Writing Intersectional Identities: Keywords for Creative Writers* (New York: Bloomsbury Academic, 2019).

Aesop. "Androcles and the Lion." Folklore and Mythology Electronic Texts. https://sites.pitt.edu/~dash/type0156.html (accessed July 24, 2024).

"Albany Movement." Martin Luther King, Jr. Encyclopedia. Martin Luther King, Jr. Research & Education Institute. Stanford University. https://kinginstitute.stanford.edu/encyclopedia/albany-movement (accessed September 26, 2021).

"An Affair of Honor." Directed by Sheree Folkson. *Bridgerton* (Shondaland, 2020).

"AP Latin." College Board. https://apcentral.collegeboard.org/courses/ap-latin (accessed June 19, 2023).

Apicella, Coren L. and Joan B. Silk. "The Evolution of Human Cooperation." *Current Biology* 29, no. 11 (June 2019), r477–r450.

Aristophanes. *Lysistrata*, translated by George Theodoridis (Poetry in Translation, 2000). https://www.poetryintranslation.com/PITBR/Greek/Lysistrata.php (accessed September 24, 2024).

Asimov, Isaac. *Foundation; Foundation and Empire; Second Foundation* (New York: Alfred A. Knopf, 2010).

Atwood, Margaret. "Some Very Basic Basics About Writing Novels." *In the Writing Burrow*, November 22, 2022. https://margaretatwood.

substack.com/p/some-very-basic-basics-about-writing (accessed September 24, 2024).

Austen, Jane. *Persuasion* (New York: Tor, 1999).

Austin, III, Lloyd J. "Statement by Secretary of Defense Lloyd J. Austin III on Tackling the Climate Crisis at Home and Abroad." U.S. Department of Defense, January 27, 2021. https://www.defense.gov/News/Releases/Release/Article/2484504/statement-by-secretary-of-defense-lloyd-j-austin-iii-on-tackling-the-climate-cr/ (accessed September 24, 2024).

Bennett, Eric. *Workshops of Empire: Stegner, Engle, and American Creative Writing during the Cold War* (Iowa City, IA: University of Iowa Press, 2015).

Big Fish. Directed by Tim Burton (Columbia Pictures, 2003).

Booth, Wayne C. *The Rhetoric of Fiction*, 2nd ed. (Chicago: University of Chicago Press, 1983).

Bordwell, David. *The Way Hollywood Tells It: Story and Style in Modern Movies* (Berkeley, CA: University of California Press, 2006).

Borislavov, Rad. "Poetics." The Chicago School of Media Theory. University of Chicago. https://csmt.uchicago.edu/glossary2004/poetics.htm (accessed October 14, 2022).

Burnett, W. R. *The Asphalt Jungle* (London: Prion Books, 1999).

Burns, Stewart, ed. *Daybreak of Freedom: The Montgomery Bus Boycott* (Chapel Hill, NC: University of North Carolina Press, 1997).

Burton, Rebecca. "The Choice." *Abyss & Apex* no. 79 (June 4, 2021). https://www.abyssapexzine.com/2021/06/the-choice/ (accessed September 24, 2024).

Butcher, S. H. *Aristotle's Theory of Poetry and Fine Art: With a Critical Text and Translation of the Poetics*, 4th ed. with corrections (London: Macmillan and Co., 1911).

Butler, Judith. *The Force of Nonviolence: An Ethico-Political Bind* (New York: Verso, 2020).

"campaign, n." *Oxford English Dictionary*, OED Online (Oxford University Press). https://doi.org/10.1093/OED/1126270477 (accessed December 2023).

"The Caper." TV Tropes. https://tvtropes.org/pmwiki/pmwiki.php/Main/TheCaper (accessed September 26, 2021).

Carroll, Lewis. *The Annotated Alice*, introduction and notes by Martin Gardner (New York: New American Library, 1960).

Cars. Directed by John Lasseter and Joe Ranft (Pixar, 2006).

Carter, Candice C. and Linda Pickett. *Youth Literature for Peace Education* (New York: Palgrave Macmillan, 2014).

Chatman, Seymour. *Story and Discourse: Narrative Structure in Fiction and Film* (Ithaca, NY: Cornell University Press, 1978).

Chenoweth, Erica. *Civil Resistance: What Everyone Needs to Know* (New York: Oxford University Press, 2021).

Cobb Jr., John B. *God and the World* (Philadelphia: Westminster Press, 1969).

Cohen, Alex. Untitled. *Tiny Snek Comics*, August 6, 2018. https://www.instagram.com/p/BmJWHGQDsC3/ (accessed September 24, 2024).

"The Con." TV Tropes. https://tvtropes.org/pmwiki/pmwiki.php/Main/TheCon (accessed September 26, 2021).

Confidence. Directed by James Foley (Lions Gate Films, 2003).

Cooper, Brenda. "For the Snake of Power." *The Weight of Light: A Collection of Solar Futures*, edited by Joey Eschrich and Clark A. Miller (Tempe, AZ: Arizona State University, 2018), 43–59.

Corvasce, Mauro V. and Joseph R. Paglino. *Modus Operandi: A Writer's Guide to How Criminals Work* (Cincinnati, OH: Writer's Digest Books, 1995).

Cowan, Geoffrey. *See No Evil: The Backstage Battle over Sex and Violence in Television* (New York: Simon and Schuster, 1979).

Crazy Rich Asians. Directed by Jon M. Chu (Warner Brothers, 2018).

Dennett, Joann Temple. "Not to Say is Better Than to Say: How Rhetorical Structure Reflects Cultural Context in Japanese-English Technical Writing." *IEEE Transactions on Professional Communication* 31, no. 3 (September 1998), 116–19.

Dickens, Charles. *A Christmas Carol* (New York: Weathervane Books, 1977).

Drash, Wayne. "Driven to Death by Phone Scammers." CNN, October 7, 2015. https://www.cnn.com/2015/10/07/us/jamaica-lottery-scam-suicide/index.html (accessed September 24, 2024).

"duel, n." *Oxford English Dictionary*, OED Online (Oxford University Press). https://doi.org/10.1093/OED/8732036001 (accessed July 2023).

Egri, Lajos. *The Art of Creative Writing* (New York: Citadel Press, 1995).

Egri, Lajos. *The Art of Dramatic Writing: Its Basis in the Creative Interpretation of Human Motives* (New York: Simon and Schuster, 1946).

Eichenwald, Kurt. *Conspiracy of Fools: A True Story* (New York: Broadway Books, 2005).

"Elderly Robocall Scam Victim Committed Suicide after 'Fraudsters' Stole Life Savings," Fox Business, July 17, 2019. https://www.foxbusiness.com/features/robocall-scam-victim-suicide-stole-life-saving (accessed September 24, 2024).

Engler, Mark and Paul Engler. *This Is an Uprising: How Nonviolent Revolt Is Shaping the Twenty-first Century* (New York: Nation Books, 2016).

Enron: The Smartest Guys in the Room. Directed by Alex Gibney (Jigsaw Productions, 2005).

Ertsgaard, Gabriel. "Narratology and Narrative Change." *The Peace Chronicle* 14.2 (Spring 2022), 51–3.

Ertsgaard, Gabriel. "Nonviolence and the Hero's Duel." SFWA Blog, June 29, 2021. https://www.sfwa.org/2021/06/29/nonviolence-and-the-heros-duel/ (accessed September 24, 2024).

Ertsgaard, Gabriel. "Solarpunk and Peace Poetics," *The Peace Chronicle* 14.2 (Spring 2022), 40–5.

Fanon, Fay. *Rip-Off: A Writer's Guide to Crimes of Deception* (Cincinnati, OH: Writer's Digest Books, 1998).

"The Features of Narrative: A Model of Narrative Form for Social Change Efforts." FrameWorks Institute, September 2021. https://www.frameworksinstitute.org/wp-content/uploads/2021/09/The-features-of-narratives.pdf (accessed September 24, 2024).

"A Feud Is a Feud." Directed by Don Weis. *The Andy Griffith Show* (Mayberry Enterprises, 1960).

Field, Syd. *The Screenwriter's Workbook* (New York: Dell Publishing, 1984).

Fisher, Roger, William Ury, and Bruce Patton. *Getting to Yes: Negotiating Agreement Without Giving In*, 3rd ed. (New York: Penguin Books, 2011).

Fontan, Victoria. *Decolonizing Peace* (Lake Oswego, OR: Dignity Press, 2012).

Forliti, Amy, and Steve Karnowski. "Chauvin gets 22½ Years in Prison for George Floyd's Death." AP News, June 25, 2021. https://apnews.com/article/derek-chauvin-sentencing-23c52021812168c579b3886f8139c73d (accessed September 24, 2024).

Frazer, Diane. "Private and Confidential." *Alfred Hitchcock's Happiness is a Warm Corpse* (New York: Dell Publishing, 1969), 168–78.

Freeman, Jan. "Toile and Trouble." *The Boston Globe*, October 13, 2002.

Freytag, Gustav. *Freytag's Technique of the Drama: An Exposition of Dramatic Composition and Art*, 5th ed., translated by Elias J. MacEwan (New York: Scott Foresman and Company, 1894).

Friedman, Gary and Jack Himmelstein. *Challenging Conflict: Mediation Through Understanding* (Chicago, IL: American Bar Association, 2008).

Fromm, Erich. *The Art of Loving* (New York: Perennial Classics, 2000).

Frozen. Directed by Chris Buck and Jennifer Lee (Disney, 2006).

Gerke, Jeff. *Plot versus Character: A Balanced Approach to Writing Great Fiction* (Cincinnati, OH: Writer's Digest Books, 2010).

Get Hard. Directed by Etan Cohen (Warner Brothers, 2015).

Gandhi, M. K. *The Selected Works of Mahatma Gandhi*, vol. 3: *The Basic Works*, edited by Shriman Narayan (Ahmedabad, India: Navajivan Publishing House, 1968).

Ghostbusters. Directed by Ivan Reitman (Columbia Pictures, 1984).

The Godfather. Directed by Francis Ford Coppola (Paramount Pictures, 1972).

The Godfather: Part II. Directed by Francis Ford Coppola (Paramount Pictures, 1974).

The Godfather: Part III. Directed by Francis Ford Coppola (Paramount Pictures, 1990).

Goodman, Tanya. *Staging Solidarity: Truth and Reconciliation in a New South Africa* (Boulder, CO: Paradigm Publishers, 2009).

Grahame, Kenneth. "The Reluctant Dragon." *The Oxford Book of Modern Fairy Tales*, edited by Alison Lurie (New York: Oxford University Press, 1993), 182–202.

Gundy, Jeff. "Literature, Nonviolence, and Nonviolent Teaching." *Teaching Peace: Nonviolence and the Liberal Arts*, edited by J. Denny Weaver and Gerald Biesecker-Mast (New York: Rowman & Littlefield, 2003), 125–36.

Hare Trigger. Directed by Friz Freleng (Warner Brothers, 1945).

Healey, Steve. "Beyond the Literary: Why Creative Literacy Matters." *Key Issues in Creative Writing*, edited by Dianne Donnely and Graeme Harper (Bristol, UK: Multilingual Matters, 2013), 48–78.

Healey, Steve. "Creative Literacy Pedagogy." *Creative Writing Pedagogies for the Twenty-First Century*, edited by Alexandria Peary and Tom C. Hunley (Carbondale, IL: Southern Illinois University Press, 2015), 169–93.

Healey, Steve. "The Rise of Creative Writing & the New Value of Creativity." *The Writer's Chronicle*, February 2009. Reprinted as "Movement 1.0 Thinking Outside Creative Writing" in Steve Healey, *The Rise of Creative Writing and the New Value of Creativity* (doctoral dissertation), University of Minnesota, 2009. https://conservancy.umn.edu/server/api/core/bitstreams/23aee473-97db-439b-82db-6cd2eee40d0e/content (accessed September 24, 2024).

Hill, Evan, Ainara Tiefenthäler, Christiaan Triebert, Drew Jordan, Haley Willis, and Robin Stein. "How George Floyd was Killed in Police Custody." *The New York Times*, May 31, 2020, updated September 7, 2021. https://www.nytimes.com/2020/05/31/us/george-floyd-investigation.html (accessed September 24, 2024).

Homer. *The Iliad*, translated by Robert Fagles (New York: Penguin Books, 1990).

Homer. *The Odyssey*, translated by Robert Fagles (New York: Penguin Books, 1996).

"The House of Quark." Directed by Les Landau. *Star Trek: Deep Space Nine* (Paramount, 1994).

"How the Toilet Got Its Name." Merriam-Webster.com. https://www.merriam-webster.com/words-at-play/word-history-of-toilet (accessed October 14, 2022).

Kahane, Adam. *Power and Love: A Theory and Practice of Social Change* (San Francisco: Berrett-Koehler Publishers, 2010).

King, Jr., Martin Luther. *Stride Toward Freedom: The Montgomery Story* (New York: Ballantine Books, 1958).

King Jr., Martin Luther. *Strength to Love* (New York: Harper & Row, 1963).

King, Jr., Martin Luther. *Why We Can't Wait* (New York: Signet Books, 1964).

Konnikova, Maria. *The Confidence Game: Why We Fall for It Every Time* (New York: Viking, 2016).

Kurlansky, Mark. *Nonviolence: The History of a Dangerous Idea* (New York: Modern Library, 2006).

Lage Raho Munna Bhai. Directed by Rajkumar Hirani (Vinod Chopra Productions, 2006).

Lakey, George. *How We Win: A Guide to Direct Action Campaigning* (New York: Melville House, 2018).

Lao Tzu. *Tao Te Ching*, translated by A. S. Kline (Poetry in Translation, 2003).

Lederach, John Paul. *The Little Book of Conflict Transformation* (New York: Good Books, 2003).

The LEGO Movie. Directed by Christopher Miller and Phil Lord (Warner Brothers, 2014).

Leigh, John. *Touché: The Duel in Literature* (Cambridge, MA: Harvard University Press, 2015).

Leverage. Created by Chris Downey and John Rogers (Electric Entertainment, 2008–12).

Lodge, Hanna. "Review: Wonder Woman Soars but Doesn't Stick the Landing." *The Beat*, May 30, 2017. https://www.comicsbeat.com/review-wonder-woman-soars/ (accessed September 24, 2024).

Love, Actually. Directed by Richard Curtis (Universal Pictures, 2003).

Manekin, Devorah and Tamar Mitts. "Effective for Whom? Ethnic Identity and Nonviolent Resistance." *American Political Science Review* 116, no. 1 (2022), 161–80. https://doi.org/10.1017/S0003055421000940.

Maurer, David. *The Big Con: The Story of the Confidence Man* (New York: MJF Books, 1999).

McLean, Bethany and Peter Elkind. *The Smartest Guys in the Room: The Amazing Rise and Scandalous Fall of Enron*, 10th anniversary ed. (New York: Penguin Books, 2013).

McQuade, Joseph. "The Forgotten Violence That Helped India Break Free From Colonial Rule." *The Independent*, November 10, 2016. https://www.independent.co.uk/world/the-forgotten-violence-that-helped-india-break-free-from-colonial-rule-a7409066.html (accessed September 24, 2024).

Mean Streets. Directed by Martin Scorsese (Warner Brothers, 1973).

Montgomery, Kathryn C. *Target Prime Time: Advocacy Groups and the Struggle over Entertainment Television* (New York: Oxford University Press, 1989).

Moon, Claire. *Narrating Political Reconciliation: South Africa's Truth and Reconciliation Commission* (Lanham, MD: Lexington Books, 2009).

Moore, Christopher W. *The Mediation Process: Practical Strategies for Resolving Conflict*, 4th ed. (San Francisco, CA: Jossey-Bass, 2014).

Morgulis, Eugene. "The Stubbornness of Wizards." *Fantasy Scroll Magazine* no. 13 (June 2016), 19–28.

"Mr. Denton on Doomsday." Directed by Allen Reisner. *The Twilight Zone* (CBS, 1959).

"Narrative Change: A Working Definition (and Some Related Terms)." Narrative Initiative, May 15, 2019. https://narrativeinitiative.org/blog/narrative-change-a-working-definition-and-related-terms/ (accessed September 24, 2024).

The New Oxford Annotated Bible (New Revised Standard Version), 5th ed. (New York: Oxford University Press, 2018).

Nicholson, Vincent D. *Cooperation and Coercion as Methods of Social Change* (Wallingford, PA: Pendle Hill, 1934).

Nolan-Haley, Jacqueline M. *Alternative Dispute Resolution in a Nutshell*, 4th ed. (St. Paul, MN: West Academic Publishing, 2013).

Ocean's Eleven. Directed by Steven Soderbergh (Warner Brothers, 2001).

Parker, Theodore. "Of Justice and the Conscience." *Ten Sermons on Religion* (first published in 1853). Wikisource. https://en.wikisource.org/wiki/Ten_Sermons_of_Religion (accessed September 24, 2024).

Parks, Rosa, with Jim Haskins. *Rosa Parks: My Story* (New York: Puffin Books, 1992).

Paullin, Theodore. *Introduction to Non-Violence* (Philadelphia, PA: The Pacifist Research Bureau, 1944).

Perrault, Charles. "Little Red Riding Hood." Folklore and Mythology Electronic Texts. https://sites.pitt.edu/~dash/perrault02.html (accessed June 26, 2024).

Phalen, Anthony. "Brazilian Priests Intervene Nonviolently to Prevent Violence, 1968." Global Nonviolent Action Database. Swarthmore College, November 18, 2009. https://nvdatabase.swarthmore.edu/content/brazilian-priests-intervene-nonviolently-prevent-violence-1968 (accessed September 24, 2024).

Pirates of the Caribbean: Curse of the Black Pearl. Directed by Gore Verbinski (Disney, 2003).

"A Poet by any Other Name." Merriam-Webster.com. https://www.merriam-webster.com/words-at-play/the-history-of-the-word-poet (accessed October 14, 2022).

The Pursuit of Happyness. Directed by Gabriele Muccino (Columbia Pictures, 2006).

Quinn, Julia. *The Duke and I* (New York: HarperCollins, 2000).

Rambo, Cat. "Big Rural," *The Weight of Light: A Collection of Solar Futures*, edited by Joey Eschrich and Clark A. Miller (Tempe, AZ: Arizona State University, 2018), 107–20.

Robinson, Jo Ann Gibson. *The Montgomery Bus Boycott and the Women Who Started It* (Knoxville, TN: University of Tennessee Press, 1987).

Robot Jox. Directed by Stuart Gordan (Empire Pictures, 1990).

Schirch, Lisa. *The Little Book of Strategic Peacebuilding* (Intercourse, PA: Good Books, 2004).

Selma. Directed by Ava DuVernay (Plan B Entertainment, 2014).

Shakespeare, William. *The Handy-Volume Shakespeare* (New York: George Routledge and Sons, *c.* 1910).

Sharp, Gene. *Power and Struggle: The Politics of Nonviolent Action, Part One* (Boston, MA: Porter Sargent Publishers, 1973).

Sharp, Gene. *The Methods of Nonviolent Action: The Politics of Nonviolent Action, Part Two* (Boston, MA: Porter Sargent Publishers, 1973).

Sharp, Gene. *The Dynamics of Nonviolent Action: The Politics of Nonviolent Action, Part Three* (Boston, MA: Porter Sargent Publishers, 1973).

Sleeping Beauty. Directed by Clyde Geromini (Disney, 1959).

Smith, Gail K. "Who Was That Masked Woman?: Gender and Form in Louisa May Alcott's Confidence Stories," in *American Women Short Story Writers: A Collection of Critical Essays*, edited by Julie Brown (New York: Garland Publishing, 1995), 45–59.

"South Africa." *Encyclopedia Britannica*. https://www.britannica.com/place/South-Africa (accessed September 19, 2021).

The Sting. Directed by George Roy Hill (Universal Pictures, 1973).

Tomlinson, Paul. *Crime Thriller: How to Write Detective, Noir, Caper & Heist, Gangster, & Police Procedurals* (independently published, 2019).

"Top Lifetime Grosses." Box Office Mojo. https://www.boxofficemojo.com/chart/ww_top_lifetime_gross/ (accessed September 27, 2023).

Torgerson, Ellen. "Violence Takes a Beating." *TV Guide*, June 4, 1977, 6–9.

Trading Places. Directed by John Landis (Paramount Pictures, 1983).

"truth, n. and adv. (and int.)." *Oxford English Dictionary*, OED Online (Oxford University Press). https://www.oed.com/view/Entry/207026 (accessed September 2021).

Vogler, Christopher. *The Writer's Journey: Mythical Structures for Writers*, 2nd ed. (Studio City, CA: Michael Wiese Productions, 1998).

Wadlington, Warwick. *The Confidence Game in American Literature* (Princeton, NJ: Princeton University Press, 1975).

Wallace, Daniel. *Big Fish: A Novel of Mythic Proportions* (Chapel Hill, NC: Algonquin Books, 1998).

Weil, Simone. *The Iliad or The Poem of Force* (Wallingford, PA: Pendle Hill, 1956).

Weiland, K. M. *Creating Character Arcs: The Masterful Author's Guide to Uniting Story Structure, Plot, and Character Development* (South Yorkshire, UK: PenForASword Publishing, 2016).

"What's in a Frame?" FrameWorks Institute, July 16, 2020. https://www.frameworksinstitute.org/article/whats-in-a-frame/ (accessed September 24, 2024).

Whitehead, Alfred North. *Religion in the Making* (New York: The Macmillan Company, 1926).

"Will Gets a Job." Directed by Ellen Gittlesohn. *The Fresh Prince of Bel-Air* (The Stuffed Dog Company, 1991).

Wink, Walter. *Engaging the Powers: Discernment and Resistance in a World of Domination* (Minneapolis, MN: Augsburg Fortress, 1992).

Wink, Walter. *When the Powers Fall: Reconciliation and the Healing of the Nations* (Minneapolis, MN: Augsburg Fortress, 1998).

Wodehouse, P. G. *Carry On, Jeeves* (New York: Penguin Books, 1956).

Wonder Woman. Directed by Patty Jenkins (Warner Brothers, 2017).

Wright, Will. *Sixguns and Society: A Structural Study of the Western* (Berkeley, CA: University of California Press, 1975).

Yang, Jeff. "The Symbolism of Crazy Rich Asians' Pivotal Mahjong Scene, Explained." *Vox*, August 31, 2018. https://www.vox.com/first-person/2018/8/17/17723242/crazy-rich-asians-movie-mahjong (accessed September 24, 2024).

Young, Art. *Shelley and Nonviolence* (The Hague: Mouton, 1975).

INDEX